T0003764

Coffee

by Major Cohen

for
dummies®
A Wiley Brand

Coffee For Dummies®

Published by: **John Wiley & Sons, Inc.,** 111 River Street, Hoboken, NJ 07030-5774, www.wiley.com

Copyright © 2021 by John Wiley & Sons, Inc., Hoboken, New Jersey

Published simultaneously in Canada

For general information on our other products and services, please contact our Customer Care Department within the U.S. at 877-762-2974, outside the U.S. at 317-572-3993, or fax 317-572-4002. For technical support, please visit https://hub.wiley.com/community/support/dummies.

Wiley publishes in a variety of print and electronic formats and by print-on-demand. Some material included with standard print versions of this book may not be included in e-books or in print-on-demand. If this book refers to media such as a CD or DVD that is not included in the version you purchased, you may download this material at http://booksupport.wiley.com. For more information about Wiley products, visit www.wiley.com.

Library of Congress Control Number: 2020952999

ISBN: 978-1-119-67901-1

ISBN: 978-1-119-67904-2 (ebk); ISBN: 978-1-119-67905-9 (ebk)

Manufactured in the United States of America

SKY10025629_031521

Contents at a Glance

Table of Contents

Introduction

Coffee has been around a long time, but the past 50 years have witnessed a monumental transition. I've spent most of my life drinking coffee, instructing others photography, and teaching coffee. I've lived through this dramatic change as specialty coffee has made drinking coffee so much more nuanced.

You may have encountered a virtually foreign language, extensive paraphernalia, and an often occurring, kind of know-it-all arrogance by some people when you're buying beans and beverages. Trying to navigate and understand the world of coffee doesn't seem to get any easier.

Yes, coffee can include not only cream and sugar, but also confusion, a multitude of questions, and even misleading marketing to name just a few, and that's a shame. But with a bit of curiosity and minimal effort, you can start to increase your coffee confidence and feel better about the ordering language, the broad and remote world where coffee comes from, and even your own at-home barista skills.

As soon as you realize and embrace it, the wonderful world of coffee can make for joyous discovery and endless enjoyment. That world — growing it, processing it, roasting it, brewing it, and on and on — is always changing, growing, and adapting. Get ready for a ride that will help you fully appreciate this miraculous thing called coffee.

About This Book

Coffee For Dummies covers a wide range of the ever-changing and broad world of coffee and what I think is important to know. I cover some of these topics within these pages:

>> **The history of coffee:** You can find out when and where coffee began and what has happened in its centuries of existence. The history of coffee is rich with intrigue, romance, and innovation.

>> **Sourcing coffee:** Coffee comes from quite a few interesting places in the world and where you're living probably isn't one of them. Growers and buyers meet up in some remote parts of the world as they begin the process of supplying coffee. Understanding what they do can help explain a lot about why coffee tastes a certain way or why you may like one coffee over another.

>> **Roasting coffee:** Sourcing delivers the green coffee bean into a roaster's hands. Without those roasters you'd just have a hard green coffee bean. The roaster is the scientist and artist whose skill is transforming that green bean into what can be ground, brewed, and enjoyed. Knowing about roasting explains a lot about your coffee likes and dislikes.

>> **Preparing coffee and espresso:** The final moments for the roasted coffee beans are most important. Although it sometimes seems that a great deal goes into making the end product in the best way — one that highlights all that the coffee has to offer — it's really rather a simple process.

>> **Looking at coffee today:** Some intriguing and courageous people have helped build the foundation of today's coffee world and getting to know a few of them helps to explain that world and can also help you make your decisions about coffee. If your curiosity is piqued and that coffee world is increasingly intriguing, you can read about ideas where you might turn next.

This book intends to share just what you need to know about coffee so you can appreciate it more. The bottom line is to help you make an even greater tasting coffee than you're creating today and to share some additional information pathways for you to explore. I clarify the coffee jargon and explain the terms baristas and coffee aficionados use so you can understand them. I've based the content on my experiences as a coffee lover and consumer, and on my experiences I've had as a coffee teacher.

Foolish Assumptions

I assume you're exploring this book for at least one of these reasons:

>> You don't know too much about coffee, but you want to find out more.

>> You do know something about coffee, perhaps more than most people, but you recognize there is so much more, and you want to understand some of that other stuff.

>> You want to figure out how to brew the perfect cup of coffee or shot of espresso to share with your friends and family.

>> You're well-informed about coffee, but you've recognized you could discover more.

Icons Used in This Book

The pictures in the margins of this book are called icons, and they point out different types of information.

TIP

This icon points outs text that can enhance either your knowledge, skill, or craftsmanship.

REMEMBER

This icons marks those helpful tidbits of info you can ponder again and again as your coffee knowledge expands.

WARNING

I've been shocked (yes, real electricity shocked) and burned, and I call out a risk or two to help you avoid the same mistakes I've made. Keep an eye out for this symbol, especially in brewing.

ON THE WEB

This icon points out interesting chunks of information you can find online about different aspects of coffee.

TECHNICAL STUFF

This world of coffee can be intensely complex, but sometimes the line between knowing and geeking out needs a bit of clarification. This icon notes info that may be super interesting, but it's not essential to understand what you need to know about everything coffee.

Where to Go from Here

This book is an easy-to-use reference. You don't have to read it from cover to cover for it to make sense and be useful to you. Simply turn to the chapter or section that interests you and dig in. If you want an overview of all things coffee, start with Chapter 1, so you're grounded in the big picture.

If a new café or coffee shop in your neighborhood is an imminent destination and the drink names have been a stumbling block, turn to Chapter 12. If you have an upcoming trip scheduled and coffee touring might be possible in the city in which you're headed, check out Chapter 16 to see if your destination is on my list. Or, if you want to brew your own coffee or espresso, go to Part 5. If you're not sure where to begin, scan the Table of Contents or index, find a topic that piques your interest, and start there. If you simply have an insatiable curiosity about some aspect of coffee beyond all the others, dive in anywhere you want.

For additional information online, check out www.dummies.com and search for the "Coffee For Dummies Cheat Sheet" to find a resource you can refer to again and again.

1
Getting Started with Coffee

Understand the basics of coffee, including where coffee beans are grown, how coffee is roasted, how you can make a great cup of coffee, and more.

Satisfy some of your most pressing questions about coffee's taste and where it comes from.

Travel to a coffee farm and encounter a by-product of processing that isn't coffee but reveals a key element important in modern coffee farming.

Clarify some of those coffee shop terms that may have confused you so you can simplify buying coffee.

Chapter **1**

Demystifying Coffee: Just the Basics

C offee and all that its world encompasses today can be confusing. I toss the word *coffee* around rather cavalierly and use it to define quite a few things — a drink, a bean, a crop, an industry. It used to be far easier, and if you're old enough, you probably remember the biggest decision was whether you wanted cream and sugar or black. The story is quite different today as the industry has exploded and, in that growth, it has become immensely confusing. I want to make it easier so you just might start to understand it better, gain a bit more confidence with it, and in the end, enjoy that coffee experience way more.

This chapter serves as your jumping-off point into the world of coffee. Whether you like it with cream and sugar, with just a little cream, with steamed milk, with some syrup and whipped cream, or just black, you can find the basics in this chapter and then dive into the rest of this book for more details in your search of the perfect cup.

Understanding What Coffee Is (and Isn't)

Coffee is right up near the top of the list of the most consumed beverages in the world. (It actually ranks third behind water and tea.) But before it gets to your cup, it's a significant, globally grown agricultural crop that represents a livelihood to millions of people around the world.

Coffee is all the following:

>> A seed (the bean), well protected in a layered fruit (the cherry).

>> Put through one of a number of distinct processes in order to get to the seed at the center. Whichever process is used plays a big part in its eventual taste. (Refer to Chapter 2 for more about the different processes and how they can affect the taste of coffee.)

>> An annual crop — and, like wine, a different crop every year, even if it's from the same place. (The chapters in Part 3 look at the different places in the world where coffee is grown.)

>> Significantly impacted by environmental conditions, such as temperature, rainfall, and where it grows. Refer to Chapter 2 for more info on coffee growing and the impact the environment has on it.

Coffee isn't any of the following:

>> Easy to grow.

>> Easy to harvest and process.

Chapter 2 explains in greater detail how coffee is grown, harvested, and processed to show you how delicate the multiple steps are that get the bean from inside the cherry.

Appreciating Coffee — from Its Past to Today

To better understand coffee today, it's useful to look at where it came from. With a history spanning across centuries as well as the globe, coffee is more easily understood when you know some of its historical background. That history has witnessed romance, revolution, discovery, and turbulent change, all of which have led to coffee being what it is today. The following sections give you a snapshot of important historical developments that have led the coffee industry to its present state.

A world of farms and fickle crops

At its most basic, coffee is a precious miracle of nature. Although it's scientifically classified in a rather confusing hierarchy of names, here I focus on two types of coffee crops:

>> **Arabica:** Represents about 70 percent of what is grown and consumed around the world and is the type seen most prominently in the gourmet or specialty coffee business. Arabica is difficult to grow because it needs elevation and is easily impacted by insects and disease. Even if everything goes perfectly in a crop year, the yield with Arabica is limited. Arabica is the type that has the best taste though, with complexities and flavors that are unrivaled.

>> **Robusta:** This would be the ideal type of coffee because it has greater yield per tree than Arabica, isn't as susceptible to insects or disease, and grows at any elevation. Unfortunately, it's known for its harsh taste characteristics, and even though a significant quantity is grown, processed, and consumed, it isn't considered specialty or gourmet.

Chapter 2 digs in to the specifics of the fruit and delves deeper into the differences between Arabica and Robusta.

The cherry is picked annually, and it yields seeds. About 95 to 97 percent of the time, each fruit has two seeds; 3 to 5 percent of the time, it has a peaberry. A *peaberry* is the seed of a cherry that has only grown one inside. Multiple decisions regarding growing, often driven by long-standing practices, availability of water, and technology, determine how the trees are raised, how their fruit is collected, and finally how the seed inside that fruit, the coffee bean, is handled. These factors all have a significant impact on the taste of the coffee when it gets to you, the consumer.

Going back to coffee's roots

An almost inadvertent discovery by some goats and their herdsman might just have started it all. Whether this story is truth or fable, the centuries that followed that discovery certainly saw coffee rise as a brewed beverage that inspired passionate interest and dialog.

Religious leaders, politicians, and artists played a part in the development of the beverage's refinement and a burgeoning café society. Cultures across time and the globe seem to have been imbued with coffee and its side effects. Furthermore, industrial and cultural revolutions, coupled with the growth of coffee consumption across all demographics, put coffee at the forefront of change. An industry sprang up from those changes as entrepreneurs recognized a wide-open frontier and major opportunities. Chapter 3 examines the history of coffee — where people started drinking it and how the business of coffee started.

Examining coffee and roasting today

Coffee in modern times really began with a vision and a dream in the late 1960s. A transition occurred that involved a small group of entrepreneurs taking a different approach. Specifically they began focusing on origin (where the coffee is grown), quality, craft roasting, and taste as fundamental to their coffee work. Like many entrepreneurial adventures, that of coffee is wonderfully woven into a kind of art and science, and roasting coffee is central to and representative of that. I discuss how coffee roasting has evolved in Chapters 9 and 10.

Traveling Worldwide — Where Coffee Is Grown

I realized early in my journey with coffee that I was challenged by global geography. The equator and the continents were easy to recognize, but the names and locations of countries, borders, mountains, lakes, and streams quickly became overwhelming as I learned more about coffee. I also found that geography established connections to the perceived quality and inherent characteristics linked to taste.

Add to all that the crucial environmental elements, because growing coffee requires Mother Nature's cooperation. The following are important aspects of climate:

>> Temperature

>> Rainfall

>> Soil conditions

>> Sun, shade, and wind

I survey these aspects in greater detail in Chapter 5. Meanwhile, the following sections look at where coffee is grown in the world to help you understand how many places coffee comes from.

Visiting the Western Hemisphere

In the Americas, coffee has been grown successfully in several countries, both large and small. Chapter 6 provides more in-depth information about these places.

Central America

Some of these smaller countries feature a few of the most noteworthy coffees and coffee success stories of the last century:

>> **Costa Rica:** Known as the Switzerland of Central America, Costa Rica offers a perfect environment for growing coffee. Peace and neutrality have allowed for the development and growth of an envied coffee infrastructure. Figure 1-1 shows a Costa Rican coffee farm.

>> **El Salvador:** Societal development, the coffee industry, and cultural growth in El Salvador both benefited and suffered together over the past 25 years, and a solid but still not fully realized coffee opportunity exists there.

>> **Guatemala:** This country is the source of some of the most exquisite and treasured coffees in the world.

>> **Honduras:** This country has a burgeoning coffee industry and an increasing premium crop production.

>> **Mexico:** One of the world's top ten coffee producers, Mexico features diverse, mountainous terrain and an equally diverse range of potential flavor profiles.

>> **Nicaragua:** Although coffee is a principal crop in Nicaragua, an opportunity remains for both increased output and better quality.

>> **Panama:** The famed Boquete Valley, and an interest and investment in producing the Geisha varietal, have cemented Panama's reputation for amazing coffees.

FIGURE 1-1:
Costa Rica has
great coffee
farms.

Photo by Major Cohen

South America

An almost perfect coffee–growing climate and vast land made South America a prime spot for cultivating a relatively new crop all the way back in the 1700s. Today it's home to Brazil and Colombia, the top coffee producers in the world for annual production. Here are countries in South American known for coffee production:

>> **Bolivia:** A forest called the Yungas in the Andes Mountains is home to some strikingly beautiful, high-elevation coffee farms. Despite Bolivia having a past reputation for lower-quality output, the industry is watching and waiting to see what the future holds.

>> **Brazil:** The largest coffee producer hasn't always been the best, but Brazil has focused on fine-tuning its crops; some prodigious infrastructure efforts and a significant goal to be a top premium coffee source have spurred a resurgence.

>> **Colombia:** Famous thanks to stellar marketing and some beautiful coffees, Colombia is thought by many to be "the most coffee" of coffees when it comes to flavor in the cup.

>> **Ecuador:** Small farms in the Andes are producing limited quantities, but there's currently hope for infrastructure investment, because coffee in Ecuador has considerable potential.

>> **Peru:** A diversity of growing regions in this country has resulted in a wide variety of intriguing flavor profiles.

>> **Venezuela:** At one time, Venezuela had a coffee output that was comparable to its high-production neighbors. However, Venezuela's diminishing output has really taken away from the country's coffee exports, and so most of the interesting and good-quality crop is consumed in country.

The Islands

With striking mountainous regions and situated perfectly in the tropical climate of the equatorial belt, these islands have history and heritage in coffee. Three are in the Caribbean Sea and one is in the Pacific Ocean, but all continue to have tremendous potential and some considerable pedigree as coffee growing origins:

>> **Cuba:** Although Cuba has been growing coffee since the mid-18th century, the political situation has all but eliminated any output from what is a coffee-growing environment with true potential.

>> **Dominican Republic:** This is another country with a long-established history of coffee farming and recognized potential for investment and renewed effort.

>> **Hawaii:** These islands host some of the most beautiful coffee farms and celebrate production of some of the most favored and pricey coffees in the world.

>> **Jamaica:** The famed Blue Mountains, which are located in the eastern third of the island, are home to coffee farms with a heritage that dates back to 1723 and French King Louis XV. King Louis sent three plants as a gift to Martinique, and five years later the governor of Martinique gave one of those as a gift to Jamaica's governor.

Heading to Africa

Home to the birthplace of coffee, and centuries later some of the most powerful stories of human perseverance and resilience, Africa today is an important frontier for innovation and growth in the coffee industry. Here are the countries in Africa that are known for coffee (Chapter 7 takes a closer look at coffee in Africa).

Northeast Africa

The Great Rift Valley, Mt. Kenya, and the Ethiopian Plateau combine to establish a splendid geography for coffee production in these two countries:

>> **Ethiopia:** The birthplace of coffee, Ethiopia is home to a long-standing, established culture that is centered on coffee and its place in community. Ethiopian coffees are some of the most exotic in the world.

>> **Kenya:** Although not the largest in terms of output among the African coffee countries, Kenya is certainly recognized and celebrated for its unusual and often high-quality, noteworthy coffees with unique flavor characteristics all their own.

Southern Africa

This region is home to countries that are often seen as having the greatest potential in the industry, as development and innovation are alive there. Following are the main coffee producers in southern Africa:

>> **Burundi:** An on-again, off-again approach has impacted Burundi's coffee consistency; despite that, this small country is often the source of some unique offerings.

>> **Congo:** Some refreshingly bright and flavorful coffees have come out of Congo in recent years.

>> **Malawi:** Despite the fact that this country has experienced turbulence linked to political instability, Malawi still has been able to export some tasty coffees that have found their way to consumers in Europe and the United States.

>> **Rwanda:** Highly respected for their response to the tragedy of genocide in the 1990s and the ensuing focus on coffee as a key to a brighter, more prosperous future, Rwandan coffee growers have established a reputation for producing some terrific coffees.

>> **Tanzania:** Mount Kilimanjaro and Mount Meru are home to some highly regarded coffee farms, and coffee plays an important role in Tanzania's economy.

>> **Zambia:** A small country with a growing interest in expanding its coffee industry, Zambia is another country with potential — one to be watched.

Heading to the Eastern Hemisphere

Perhaps the most remote and exotic environments for coffee growing exist in the region known as the Asia Pacific. Head to Chapter 8 for more information about coffee in Asia.

Consider coffee in the following countries:

>> **China:** Although coffee production in China didn't really begin in earnest until the late 1980s, what has been developed, primarily in the Yunnan Region, has been impressive, and green coffee buyers now recognize coffee from China as having huge potential.

>> **India:** An incredibly long history of both coffee and tea production has made India a long-standing and important source of both beverages.

>> **Indonesia:** The thousands of islands that make up Indonesia include a few that have established an enduring and respected place in the world of coffee.

>> **Papua New Guinea:** Coffee represents an important export for Papua New Guinea, and the industry began here with the importation of coffee seeds from the Jamaican Blue Mountains in the early 1920s.

>> **Vietnam:** The number-two coffee producer in the world, Vietnam has made progress in establishing itself as a source for quality and not just quantity over the past few decades, and so high-quality coffee exports from this country are being noted more than ever.

>> **Yemen:** Coffee dates way back to the 6th century in Yemen. The Arabian Port of Mokha, a Yemen coffee variety called Mocha, and a drink named Mocha all contribute to the confusion, but there is no denying that Yemen has been the source of some of the greatest coffees.

ROASTING: WHERE IT STARTED

Roasting has seen some incredible technical advances in the past century. At its core, this simple concept has been developed and refined since someone, long ago, realized that the coffee seed, when roasted, ground, and steeped, created a flavorful, powerful beverage. Although that realization occurred centuries ago, the industry that developed around coffee roasting took some time to get going.

A few beans tossed in a frying pan over an open fire may seem almost too elementary, but that's an appropriate way to think of the beginning of coffee roasting. Speed, efficiency, and quantity drove interim change until finally, a focus and prioritization to use the art and science for the best tastes have prevailed.

In Chapter 9, I dig into the history of roasting and the beginnings of the business that is coffee.

The Lowdown on Roasting Coffee

Take a raw, green seed, and heat it up until it turns a shade of brown. Sounds easy unless the seed is a coffee bean, and you begin to grasp the impact roasters can have on the end result (the flavor qualities and characteristics) as they ply their trade, a skilled combination of artistic creativity and sound science.

Here are the basics to roasting coffee:

>> Early roasters prioritized decisions around speed, efficiency, and economics thinking that their path from a green, raw, unroasted seed of a fruit — that is, how they might raise or lower temperature to affect the time it took to reach the color of brown they were after — was about using less fuel to heat or less time spent by the person doing the work. Not until the beginnings of specialty coffee (refer to Chapter 4) did roasters begin to understand and target the desired flavors by adjusting the time and temperature continuum and by all but ignoring the earlier priorities of speed, efficiency, and economics.

>> If great flavor is the vision and established goal, then there is neither a correct result nor a wrong one.

>> The entire process takes only minutes, but within that time frame are multitudes of decision points when the roaster draws on experience, an aesthetic connection to the process and intended goal, and a scientific expertise that drives confidence throughout a delicate dance with fire.

I jump deeper into the details of roasting in Chapter 10.

Examining Brewing

All the steps that have contributed to get the coffee bean expertly roasted are incomplete without a transition to a consumable and hopefully delicious beverage. Through brewing, coffee drinkers finally get what they're after.

The following list shows some of the ways in which coffee is brewed:

>> **Cupping:** This is the industry standard for assessing coffee. *Cupping* refers to a brewing method where precisely ground coffee is placed in contact with hot water, and extraction happens. After a carefully measured brew time, the grounds have sunk in the bowl or cup, and someone (a cupper) tastes it. Although it's a complex, somewhat impractical method for a daily morning coffee ritual, it's undeniably the best way to brew, compare, contrast, and eventually assess multiple coffee samples.

>> **French press:** Perhaps the first sophisticated brewing method, French press is an extremely popular way to brew coffee. As is the case with every brewing method, this one has benefits and drawbacks.

>> **Drip coffee:** The most ubiquitous method — because you encounter it everywhere you get coffee — drip-coffee brewing depends on gravity and a filter to deliver the end result.

Chapter 11 takes a closer look at these different brewing methods, and more.

Brewing Espresso

An amazing technological advancement in brewing developed in Italy in the early 1900s led to what is one of the most significant experiences in today's coffee scene. In simplest terms, *espresso* is strong black coffee created by forcing steamy hot water through ground coffee using pressure. This list covers a few basics about espresso:

>> Espresso got its start in a quest for speed.

>> Espresso brewing involves some sophisticated gear creating a remarkably simple but small and concentrated output: a shot of espresso that's usually 1–2 ounces.

>> The espresso world has the most well-known and unusual drinks and recipes.

Chapter 12 takes a closer look at the phenomenon that is espresso and more.

Examining Where Coffee Is Now

The world of coffee today belongs to you, me, and all other coffee drinkers. Whether it's simply a desire to easily find good-tasting coffee or a desire to dig in, explore, and realize that as a consumer that your action buying a coffee or some beans can have a more worldly impact and relevance. At its core, coffee today is about people and the vision they have for a sustainable coffee future. The following sections highlight the current state of coffee.

Identifying some of the people behind the coffee industry today

All that you experience of coffee today is a result of someone's spirit, vision, and imagination. In many cases, unsung heroes — and some well-known names, too — have impacted coffee. They've all demonstrated a mix of entrepreneurial vision, perseverance, and even a bit of craziness, and they've all inspired me.

Chapter 13 identifies some of the trailblazing companies and individuals who have played a part in making the coffee business what it is today.

Recognizing coffee's presence today

Coffee is almost everywhere you go, and you may want to replicate both the brewed coffee and espresso experiences that you enjoy at your local coffeehouse in your own home. You may have a lot of questions, ranging from how you begin and what ingredients and gear you need. Furthermore, you may be thinking about the type of business you're supporting with your purchase. Does it support the folks who do the work to grow the coffee? Is it considering the environmental impact of its efforts?

You may be surprised at the array of beans, brewers, grinders, kettles, and scales that are available. Any number of them may end up on your list, and you may even hunger for more.

Perhaps you want to read more — maybe a book, periodical, or blog. Perhaps your curiosity leads you to consider taking a class or classes. All these options and more are possible in today's world of coffee. I explain coffee's presence today in greater detail in Chapter 14.

THE COFFEE WORLD THROUGH MY EYES

I started with coffee at an early age, drank quite a lot of bad coffee in a 20-year career as a photography teacher, and landed a part-time barista job in Boston with a Seattle-based coffee start-up. Over the first seven years I experienced and learned. In 2003, I was offered an opportunity to move to Seattle and join a team of coffee educators. Coffee opened my eyes to the world.

The last decade of my career I had a chance to travel extensively as both an ambassador for Starbucks brand and as a coffee educator for Starbucks and the SCA. While traveling, I was able to meld my passions of photography with coffee, and I took thousands of photographs. My work took me to coffee farms in Central America and Sumatra, Indonesia. Hosting coffee trainings, lecturing, and doing media work took me to Japan, China, Vietnam, Cambodia, Jakarta, Taiwan, Korea, and Thailand, not to mention dozens of states in the United States I have enjoyed working in. Here are some of my favorite images from those travels.

(continued)

(continued)

Photos by Major Cohen

Here you can see a vast coffee seedling nursery on a farm in Costa Rica. The lifeblood of every farm — the nursery — is where the new trees begin (top left). Top right shows the collected cherries in a picker's basket. Hands sort the day's collection to send to the mill (middle left). Workers work in a drying patio in the Terrazu region of Costa Rica (middle right). End-of-the-day patio work collects drying coffee for overnight protection until the next day (second to last photo). Workers' belongings are hanging in a tree nearby where they're picking (bottom).

Chapter **2**

Figuring Out What Coffee Is

Coffee — the beverage you (and I) drink — is best understood if you pick a spot on a cyclical path, even though it's a kind of like which comes first, the chicken or the egg conundrum?

Using the beverage as a grounding point in this cycle, all that precedes it, all that goes into it begins with a seed. I refer to it most as a bean because what we buy in a store in a bag, what a roaster roasts, is most often described that way. But it is actually a seed and in the first stage it is planted, germinates, and a coffee tree is started.

Think of the three important stages that combine to make coffee taste the way it does:

» The miracle of nature

» The processing of the cherry into the beans that will eventually go to the roaster

» The roasting of the coffee

This chapter digs into the first two points and looks at the fruits — the coffee cherries — that grow on a tree and explains what happens to the coffee cherry from harvesting to processing. I also discuss the most common types of coffee as well as some varietals that have appeared on the scene. Part 4 focuses more on the roasting stage.

Understanding the Life Cycle of Coffee: From Seed to Bud to Cherry to Harvest

The terrain in which coffee trees grow is often hilly, remote, and at high elevations. To better grasp coffee, I focus on the life cycle and focus on some basics of coffee farming — at the beginning.

Although the exact amount of coffee produced varies year to year, coffee production as an agricultural product is remarkably consistent from season to season. World coffee production for 2019–2020 was approximately 171 million bags. *Bags* are the industry specific coffee measurement and are 132 pounds (60 kilograms each), so 171 million bags equals roughly 22 billion pounds.

After a coffee seed is planted, it takes about three to four years for it to reach maturity. Figure 2-1 illustrates the overall life cycle of a coffee, from seed to bean. Figure 2-2 shows from left to right the stages a cherry goes through from seedling to a ripe cherry. The following sections provide more detail about what happens and when.

FIGURE 2-1: The coffee-growing process, from seed to bean.

Source: Angel Dots/Shutterstock.com

Photos by Major Cohen

FIGURE 2-2:
Seedling-
flower-cherry.

Flowers appear on coffee tree branches

The flowers appear on coffee tree branches once every year just after the area's initial heavy rainy season. The flowers are jasmine-scented and a striking white color (refer to Figure 2-3 to a branch with flowers). After a few days the flowers fall off the branch leaving a single node from which the fruit, a coffee cherry, will form.

FIGURE 2-3:
A coffee tree
branch with
flowers.

Photo by Major Cohen

THE POWERFUL SMELL OF COFFEE FLOWERS

I have two vivid memoires about coffee flowers that I've carried with me for many years. Their powerful and beautiful smell and their striking visual impact are something you don't forget after you've witnessed them.

- Mary Williams often spoke about seeing the trees during that brief period when they're in full flower and compared them to seeing trees covered in fresh new snow in colder climates. (I discuss Mary more in Chapter 13.) You can just picture it — a white blanket resting on the darker green branches.

- Carlos Batres from El Salvador shared a memory passed down to him of the aroma of coffee flowers during that peak few days. The smells were so intense that winds carried them down off the mountainside across the coastline. Sailors in passing ships on the waters off the coast of El Salvador experienced it many miles from the coffee farm. (Flip to Chapter 6 for more on El Salvador.)

If you ever have the chance to visit a coffee farm and experience the smell yourself, don't hesitate.

The flowers develop into a cherry

About seven months later, the flowers develop into a fruit, referred to as a *cherry* (see flower and ripening cherries in Figure 2-4).

FIGURE 2-4: From left, a coffee tree flower to the different shades of a coffee cherry until it ripens.

Photo by Mauro Madrigal

REMEMBER

Two beans are inside that cherry — except in the rare case when only one bean develops. These rare beans are called peaberries. A *peaberry*, which gets the name because of its smaller, rounder shape looks like a pea, happens in 3 to 5 percent of all coffee. These unusual-shaped beans are often mixed right into all the other beans, and you can sometimes sort through a bag of coffee you buy and find them.

Sometimes, roasters hand sort them in the green, unroasted stage (the cherry processing has occurred, but the coffee is an unroasted bean) and sold as peaberry coffee. My experience with the taste of peaberry is that beyond the extraordinary work of hand sorting them out of processed green beans, there is little difference between normal and peaberry when it is roasted and brewed.

A team of pickers pick the cherries

The cherries are picked, usually by teams of pickers who have been sent into particular areas on a farm with abundant ripe cherries. Coffee picking begins at the peak of ripeness, but not all cherries on a branch ripen at the same time (as Figure 2-5 shows). Experienced pickers visually identify and pick the ripe cherries. Essentially like all ripe fruit, the cherry is at its sweetest because the sugars inside are at their highest levels. The pickers leave the less ripe on the branch to be picked later in the picking season.

FIGURE 2-5:
The cherries on the branch ripen at different times.

Photo by Major Cohen

REMEMBER

As soon as the cherry is twisted from the branch, the window of vulnerability begins. That means the longer the cherry sits in a basket or a pile, generally in a warm climate, the shorter it stays fresh. After all, coffee cherry is a fruit, so the goal is to keep it as fresh as possible for as long as possible.

Add in the seasonal differences around the world within the Coffee Belt (see Chapter 5 for more details), and you end up having coffee being picked in almost every month somewhere in the coffee world. It also means the period when the coffee is being picked is longer than one month. Table 2-1 breaks down when coffee is picked and where in some of the top coffee producers to give you a better idea.

TABLE 2-1   ## Coffee's Harvesting Calendar

Month	Central and South America and Caribbean	Asia Pacific	Africa
October		Indonesia: Northern Sumatra	Northern DR Congo
November	Colombia Jamaica	Indonesia Yemen	Ethiopia Kenya Uganda
December	Costa Rica Jamaica Mexico Nicaragua	China Papua New Guinea Vietnam	Ethiopia Uganda
January	Costa Rica El Salvador Guatemala Mexico Nicaragua Panama	China	
February	El Salvador Guatemala Panama		
March			
April	Northern Colombia	Indonesia: Northern Sumatra	Southern DR Congo
May	Ecuador	Papua New Guinea	Southern DR Congo Rwanda

Month	Central and South America and Caribbean	Asia Pacific	Africa
June	Southern Brazil	Papua New Guinea	Rwanda
	Colombia		
	Ecuador		
	Central Peru		
July	Brazil		
	Central Peru		
August	Northern Peru		Tanzania
September	Northern Peru		Southern DR Congo
			Ethiopia
			Tanzania
			Uganda

The pickers hand sort the picked cherries

Toward the end of the day, the pickers usually hand sort (as Figure 2-6 shows) the picked cherries to prepare them to be transported to the mill and processed.

The cherries are then transported to processing. The way the cherries get to processing varies greatly on the geography and the processing method used; think by ox-drawn wagons (see Figure 2-7), on motorbikes or bicycles, or on foot.

The cherries are processed

Processing entails removing the outer layers of skin and what is just beneath. Quite simply the steps coming turn the cherry, the fruit, into the bean, the seed, by removing these layers.

No matter whether the farm is fully integrated and the depulper site, often called the *mill*, is on the farm, or whether the farm is a member of a cooperative and the co-op mill is nearby, the freshly picked coffee cherries need to be processed within hours to limit the window of time the cherries sit before the outer layers are removed.

Photo by Major Cohen

Photo by Major Cohen

BITING INTO A COFFEE CHERRY: WHAT IT TASTES LIKE

When you bite through what is really a surprisingly thin skin of a cherry, you may notice that some of the bright red cherries seem sweeter than others. Furthermore, the cherry doesn't have much flesh or pulp. You may expect it to taste a bit like a Bing cherry, watermelon, or a seeded grape, but it doesn't have any real pulp like those fruits. However, a coffee cherry is tasty with a simple sweetness and honey-like flavor.

Refer to the section "Processing the Cherry: Getting to the Bean," later in this chapter, to find out more about the steps in the different methods of processing, including drying, storing, and so on.

Meeting the Two Main Types of Coffee and Understanding the Subspecies

Although nature has provided a complex number of variations that are coffee, there are two species groups of coffee — *Arabica* and *Robusta* — that are grown around the world and are most consumed.

TECHNICAL STUFF

Although the scientific names are complex, the family of coffee plants are the *Rubiaceae*. (Other flowering plants, including the madder and bedstraw family, are also *Rubiaceae*.) Arabica and Robusta are the two species groups.

The following takes a closer look at characteristics of these two types:

>> **Arabica:** Arabica was named around the 17th century when the bean crossed the Red Sea from Ethiopia to present day Yemen and lower Arabia. As Chapter 3 explains, those trees taken from Yemen were from the Bourbon and Typica genetic groups. Seeds and plants from those early exports represent a significant amount of what is seen today in annual production and throughout coffee production history.

   In fact, roughly 70 to 75 percent of the coffee that is cultivated in the world today is Arabica. It's the type recognized for quality and characteristics like sweetness, complexity, fruitiness that are thought to be better tasting. (Read on for more info on flavors and refer to Chapters 6, 7, and 8 for more details about taste and place.)

>> **Robusta:** Also referred to as *Canephora*, Robusta earned its name because it is easier to grow than Arabica. It's a hardy plant. Even though Robusta is certainly an important world crop because it represents 25 to 30 percent of the world coffee production, it tastes harsher.

The chapters in Part 3 identify which different geographic areas are known for growing these two types.

Arabica and Robusta have striking similarities and differences. I've stood on some farms in Sumatra where they grow virtually side by side and needed help to tell them apart. With experience I could see that the leaves and the distribution of cherry on a branch represent subtle differences. Table 2-2 compares the two to help you see the differences.

TABLE 2-2 ## Comparing Arabica and Robusta

	Arabica	Robusta
Bean size	Larger, oval-shaped bean	Smaller, rounder bean
Time to Blossom	7 to 9 months	9 to 11 months
Taste	Sweeter, softer, more complex	Stronger, harsher
Caffeine	About 0.8 to 1.5 percent	About 1.7 to 3.5 percent
Growing altitude	800 to 2,200 meters	0 to 900 meters

Robusta is a bit easier to grow, less susceptible to insects and climate anomalies, and has bigger yield per tree per season. If only it tasted as good as Arabica, it would be a far more desirable crop.

REMEMBER

I understand why people are often confused with coffee. Even though Arabica and Robusta are the two main types (or species) of coffee, each has many kinds of varieties. Think of apples to help you better understand coffee. Apples, you say? Yes. Apple is the species, and a variety of choices (the subspecies) ranging from a Granny Smith, Delicious, Pink Lady, and Gala are all examples. They're all types of apples, but they have different characteristics, variety to variety. Coffee is the same. Arabica is the main type (the species) with Typica, Bourbon, and numerous others as examples of the subspecies. Each is a type of Arabica coffee, but they all have different characteristics.

Here are a few of the more common types of Arabica:

>> **Typica** is the most prominent and is the genetic parent to many of the common Arabicas. It's high yield and generally has excellent cup profiles or tastes. Even better, it's quite susceptible to pests and disease.

>> **Bourbon** is a lower-yielding coffee. It's tougher to grow but has led to subspecies like Caturra.

>> **Caturra** is a high-yield coffee with a unique compact tree, making management and harvesting easier.

>> **Catuai** is also high yield and sturdy with compact trees.

There are more than 50 types (cultivars developed from the Arabica species) of Arabica coffee, whereas there are many less types of Robusta coffee. Some of more than 50 varieties include

>> Batian

>> Catimor

>> Costa Rica 95

>> Lempira

>> RAB C15

>> Sarchmor

>> Timor Hybrid

>> Villa Sarchi

Although both varieties (Bourbon and Typica) are prominent, coffee-growing science, known as *agronomy*, has led to the development of additional varieties in the search for plants that might be more productive, easier to cultivate, and even more resistant to potential enemies like disease and insects. These different coffees are really the result of scientific advancement; new developments are being announced often.

Processing the Cherry: Getting to the Bean

After the cherry is collected, it needs to be processed, that is the layers surrounding the actual bean must be removed, before the beans can be sent to a roaster.

The different layers that processing removes to get to the coffee bean are (refer to Figure 2-8):

>> Cherry skin

>> Mucilage

>> Parchment

>> Silverskin

Layers of the Coffee Cherry

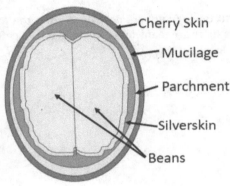

— Cherry Skin

— Mucilage

— Parchment

— Silverskin

— Beans

FIGURE 2-8: The layers of a ripe cherry removed during processing.

These sections look at the three processing methods:

>> **Washed:** Using large quantities of water

>> **Semi-washed:** Using some water, but not a lot

>> **Natural:** Using no water

I also discuss pulped natural processing, or honey processing, one variation used in coffee processing.

REMEMBER

Variations happen as coffee is processed in remote and sometimes less industrialized settings, and many of the processes are personalized and handed down through generations of family farming. As modernization has occurred, some methods are changing, and you'll often encounter combinations of old and new in a single processing environment.

As the coffee world has experienced the same information explosion as other industries have, many coffee growers and processors are exploring diverse processing methods. If word spreads that someone has achieved a considerable success with another method that impacts either taste, quality, or price, many probably will rush to replicate that new processing method to stay in front of any trend.

Washed coffee processing

Washing coffee processing, most often associated with coffees coming from Central and South America, is one of the most common ways that coffee is processed. This method uses large quantities of water to wash the cherries. Washed coffees often have cleaner taste qualities and enhanced acidity because of the removal of the outside layers, which can impact acidity and body when left coating the outside.

Here's how washed processing works in a nutshell:

1. **Collected cherries are fed into a machine called a pulper or depulper (as shown in Figure 2-9).**

   A pulper, or depulper (both terms describe the same machine and are used widely and synonymously), removes the skin, leaving thin layers of fruit/mucilage and the seed. The machine actually rips the layers off the underlying stronger layers and seed. Think of the layers of a seeded grape or Bing cherry to get an idea, although the skin and fleshy layers of coffee cherry are much thinner.

FIGURE 2-9:
A depulper in
Costa Rica.

Photo by Major Cohen

The machines can vary a great deal in size and configuration and often large facilities like you might find at a large coffee cooperative mill will have multiple depulpers.

The smallest facilities are often called *micro mills.* They're often part of fully integrated farm operations where all steps prior to and after are carried out on an individual farm.

2. **After the pulped beans are skinless but with some thin layer of mucilage and the parchment skin layer, they're carried in water channels to a tank where they rest for a time sitting in clean water.**

This fermentation step ensures that the remaining bits of material — the mucilage — are more thoroughly removed.

3. **The wet beans are then dried in the sun or in a mechanical dryer; sometimes a combination of a drying patio, table, and the mechanical dryer is used.**

They must be raked often to ensure even drying (see Figure 2-10). Sometimes a mechanical dryer is used.

FIGURE 2-10:
The beans are raked to make sure they're evenly dried.

Photo by Major Cohen

REMEMBER

4. **The beans are stored for 6 to 10 weeks.**

The end result of this processing is also referred to as *parchment dried* because the cherries' remaining layer on the bean is the parchment skin covering the underlying bean. The parchment skin provides a kind of protection or covering, and it remains on the bean for weeks as the beans are stored and rest, *reposa* in Spanish. This parchment will be dry milled off the rested green beans just prior to them being bagged and shipped.

Semi-washed processing

Coffee cherry processing using the semi-washed method begins with the cherries being depulped right after they're picked, just like the washing process. However, this method differs. Here is how the semi-washed processing method works:

1. **The picked cherries are depulped immediately (refer to Figure 2-11).**

2. **The depulped beans are gently rinsed, often by hand in buckets, as in Figure 2-12.**

FIGURE 2-11: A hand-operated depulper in Sumatra.

Photo by Major Cohen

FIGURE 2-12:
Workers in
Sumatra
handwash the
depulped beans.

Photo by Major Cohen

3. **The beans are then partially dried overnight before they're transported to a larger facility.**

4. **The beans, still wet, are hulled, stripping off the parchment layer.**

5. **The beans are then dried so that they can be stored and later shipped.**

Semi-washed processing is almost exclusive to Indonesia where it's called *giling basah*. Refer to Chapter 8 for more details about this method.

Natural processing

The natural, or dry processing, method is older and has been seen in coffee preparation from the beginning, when machines hadn't been developed to depulp. It began in Africa, probably owing its start to that less developed infrastructure and limited access to water, but today it can be seen around the world.

Here you can see what happens with this method:

1. **The cherries go directly from harvesting to drying, and the outer layers aren't removed until they have been dried out to the consistency of a raisin.**

2. **The beans are laid out in the sun either on patios or drying tables, and they must be moved frequently to foster even drying.**

REMEMBER

Natural processing is quite dependent on timing because the beans covered with all the fruit and skin can go from perfection to rotted in a short period of time.

Pulped natural or honey processing

Some places use pulped natural processing, also referred to as miel processing (*miel* is Spanish for honey) to process coffee. With this method, the skin and much of the underlying fruit layer are removed. A small amount of the mucilage is left on as the coffee dries, impacting the subsequent flavor. Pulped natural is seen primarily in Brazil.

Honey processing is more likely to come from Central American sources like Costa Rica or El Salvador. The terms black, red, or yellow honey refer to the color the bean turned as it dried, owing to the small layer of fruit material that was left on it in the partial depulping.

WHAT HAPPENS TO THE REMOVED SKIN DURING WASHED AND SEMI-WASHED PROCESSING?

In the past, the cherry skin was removed during washed and semi-washed processing, and the skin was dumped into streams and rivers to be carried away. Not very environmentally friendly. Thankfully things have changed a lot in the past 20 years. Processors saw a couple of valuable uses for what was thought to be worthless cherry skin:

- **Composting:** Processors realized composting the skin and using it to create nutrient-rich soil was beneficial and it became the widely adopted practice.

  For example, I visited a farm in Costa Rica early in my career where the farm owner, after proudly touring me through his mountainous fields and well-kept micro mill and drying patios, took me down a rocky, rutted dirt road where I smelled a distinct and increasingly pungent odor. We pulled off a side road to a 20- to 25-foot-tall pile of drying coffee cherry skin. He informed me that this pile was reasonably new and just starting as nutrient-rich compost. We walked a bit farther where he then dug a shovel into what was a clearly and older more decomposed pile full of numerous healthy earthworms. Other neighboring farm owners all processed and utilized their skin in a similar way. In cooperatives they lined up for a chance to get some of this wonderful, rich soil in the season between harvests. Often, to take advantage of the extra nutrient-rich nature of this soil, they introduced small shovelfuls at the base of every coffee tree.

(continued)

(continued)

- **Cascara:** Another new use for coffee cherry skin is cascara, from the Spanish *cáscara,* meaning husk. The skin is carefully dried and packaged so that consumers can steep it like tea. Cascara tea is slightly fruity, a bit sweet, and the brew is a lovely light pink color.

See the following photo for an example of the pile of cherry skins.

Photo by Major Cohen

2

The Story of Coffee

Appreciate the history behind coffee, including the early civilizations that started drinking coffee and how the hot drink has evolved over the centuries.

Travel to the Industrial Revolution and the early days of the coffee business to begin to understand what drove the burgeoning business of coffee.

Understand a fundamental transition in the coffee business that moves it to change priorities for some and sets up a new approach that's key to the consumer coffee experience today.

Become familiar with the global nature of today's café experience, some of the people who created and drive the business today, and a few key statistics that may surprise you.

Chapter **3**

Familiarizing Yourself with Some Coffee History

One of the first specific curiosities that arose when I began to explore coffee took me to the history of coffee. When I was thinking of changing careers a quarter century ago to coffee, a mentor told me that a great deal of her love and inspiration around coffee came from the romance and coffee's history. Now more than 25 years later I see that quite clearly.

This chapter shares some of what has inspired me in coffee's history; the history is grand and complex, and this chapter touches on a few of the historical highlights.

Understanding How Geography Is Linked to History — the Coffee Belt

To fully understand and appreciate the history of coffee, you need to explore the most basic geography of the coffee-growing world.

Coffee needs a few things to grow successfully:

>> Warm temperatures

>> Elevation

>> Adequate rainfall

>> A bit of good fortune gifted by Mother Nature

Chapter 2 discusses in great detail what coffee needs to grow. What's important to know here is how geography is so important.

Coffee was first grown in an area informally called the Coffee Belt, the equatorial band between the Tropics of Cancer and Capricorn including the equator. All the coffee in the world today is still grown in this belt. By knowing where coffee is grown (and has been grown), you can better comprehend its history. When I was early in my coffee journey, I was confused until I studied this map and could track the evolution of coffee history to today. Refer to Chapter 5 for a map of the Coffee Belt. The rest of this chapter then highlights several figures in these geographical areas that are part of coffee's history.

Looking Back at Coffee's Roots

The history of coffee is intensely rich, with romance, intrigue, cultural revolutions, and political scheming, just to name a few of the multitude of factors that have informed it. To grasp where coffee production and the industry are now, you need a basic understanding of the past. These sections discuss some of the very first instances of coffee history. You can also check out Appendix B, which is a timeline that highlights older history to the modern era.

Kaldi and his goats

The birthplace of coffee is Africa, Ethiopia specifically. Of the most recounted legendary stories of coffee's beginnings, none is more often shared than that of a poet and music-loving Ethiopian goat herder named Kaldi (he's also known as Khalid).

Kaldi's daily work took him into the fields of Ethiopia where he tended to his animals and roamed the hillsides, indulging his imagination and playing his pipe. During the day he separated from his goats; a high-pitched note from his musical instrument signaled his goats to come.

As legend has it, one day he signaled, but there was no reply, no sign that his goats had heard or were beginning to wander his way. He went in the direction they had last traveled and found them gathered around plants whose branches were covered with small, bright red, grape-sized fruits.

The goats seemed to be nibbling these cherries off the branches, and they exhibited high spirits with no intention of leaving the area. Kaldi was successful in getting them home, but he was surprised when the next day on nearing the general area, his goats had found their way back to the trees. The goats seemed energized, and Kaldi wondered about what might be occurring.

His next instinct was to try some himself. At first, he nibbled on some leaves, but their bitterness was off-putting. Next, he plucked a cherry from the branches. It was sweet but mostly seed with a small layer of flesh and skin. He slowly sensed a change as he too was becoming more alert, more energized. His poet's mind raced, and musical ideas flowed more readily than ever before.

Kaldi shared his discovery with his father and local religious leaders. Not long later word spread about the energizing brew that could be made using these berries. What Kaldi didn't know at the time was those trees were the first known coffee.

At first, the Ethiopians probably also chewed and ate the coffee fruit, but curiosity, innovation, and invention led them to both boil and include it as an ingredient, and coffee as it's known today was born.

The Ethiopians cultivated coffee for hundreds of years before Rhazes, an Arabian physician, first wrote of coffee sometime in the 10th century.

From Ethiopia to the Arabian Peninsula

Owing to the proximity of Africa and the Arabian Peninsula, conflict and trade highlight history. In the hundreds of years since Kaldi's discovery and the Ethiopian establishment of coffee, coffee infused the Arabian culture as it had the Ethiopian.

By the 1400s in Arabia, religious leaders had realized the benefits of coffee in helping them stay awake to study, discuss, and celebrate midnight services. Coffee moved from this use by religious leaders to more everyday use as the wealthy came to discover it. Muslim homes sometimes had coffee rooms where gatherings and consumption ensued.

With the Ottoman Turks in full control of the coffee center Yemen in 1536, coffee became an integral and important commodity to be traded throughout the Turkish

Empire. (Check out Chapter 8 for how Yemen continues to be a sought-after origin in coffee production.) Beans were most often shipped from the Yemeni Port of Mokha (also spelled Mocha or Mukha); coffee coming from there was given the port's name. Today people around the world sip on mocha, the name derived from this port.

The Turks were immensely protective of their virtual monopoly, and they prohibited the export of any green, unroasted coffee unless it had been subjected to boiling water or partially roasted.

Egyptian warehouses were the primary hub where French and Venetian merchants took possession of this valuable and increasingly sought-after product.

Thanks to Baba Budan, coffee appears in India

Of course, such a valuable item as fertile berries would eventually be smuggled out, and sometime around 1600 a Moslem pilgrim Baba Budan smuggled a handful of seeds by taping them to his stomach (or maybe in his beard depending on the story you encounter first).

Baba Budan had been on a pilgrimage to Mecca. As he was making his way home, he stopped in the notable Yemen port city. While there he was served a dark sweet beverage called *quahwa*. He was quite taken by the beverage; as he learned more, he realized that his Arab hosts were intensely protective of the seed from which this beverage came. In fact, it was illegal to export the seeds, so he found a way to steal seven seeds.

These seeds ended up in the Mysore mountains of India where trees were propagated.

Heading to Europe . . . and Beyond

In the late 1500s the Dutch traders transported some coffee trees from India to Holland, stopping in Ceylon (today Sri Lanka) on the way. Coffee had started to infiltrate Europe, and the American colonies weren't far behind.

At first coffee would be received poorly, but not long later it would replace other common breakfast beverages of the time, beer and wine.

The first coffeehouses open

Coffee, which was first used for its supposed medicinal benefits in the digestive system and an overall sense of wellbeing, took a while to catch on in Europe. Many initially received it somewhat skeptically as an odd-tasting, mysterious, and exotic Arabian product; however, after the wealthy made it in vogue, more and more people began drinking it. By the mid 1600s, many people consumed it.

The following sections examine a few examples of how coffee appeared in different parts of Europe.

Austria

In 1683 Austria saw the opening of its first coffeehouse. Having recently defeated the Turks in the Battle of Vienna, part of the reward was Turkish coffee. Coffee served in the early Viennese cafés included milk and sugar, the precursor to the *melange*, a well-known Viennese café favorite. Refer to Chapter 16 for more info about Viennese cafés today.

England

The first coffeehouse, named The Angel, opened in Oxford in 1652. The London coffeehouse named Pasqua Rosee quickly followed it. As a slew of openings followed, these coffeehouses gained the name *penny universities*, because the price was low for a place where vibrant conversation among spirited patrons occurred.

Quite a few of the venerable and historically significant institutions of England got their start in these penny universities. Jonathan's Coffee House, which opened in 1698, would become the London Stock Exchange. Auction houses Sotheby's and Christie's note coffeehouses as their starting points, and the famous Lloyd's of London began as Edward Lloyd's coffeehouse.

Italy

Street vendors selling lemonade added coffee to their available offerings. In 1683 Venice saw the first of what would become many coffeehouses there.

France

The Parisians enjoyed a taste of their first coffeehouse in 1672. Parisians weren't fully entrenched in coffeehouse life until 1689 when Francois Procope, an Italian immigrant, opened Café de Procope.

At first, the French enjoyed a brewed concoction that had originated from the Turks. It was boiled and described as harsh and bitter. The French created an infusion-style brewing using boiling water and ground coffee. The preparation involved using finely ground coffee suspended in a cloth bag above a carafe while boiling water was poured through the bag. What dripped through was decidedly milder than the boiled coffee version.

In addition, the French were the first to add milk to their brewed coffee, and the café au lait was born. Chapter 11 discusses different types of brewing methods for coffee in greater detail.

I've always loved this quote from famous French writer Honore de Balzac, who observed in his coffee explorations (where he evidently enjoyed consuming finely ground coffee straight up dry):

> "Everything becomes agitated. Ideas quickly march into motion like battalions of a grand army to its legendary fighting ground, and the battle rages. Memories charge in, bright flags on high; the cavalry of metaphor deploys with a magnificent gallop. Forms and shapes and characters rear up; the paper is spread with ink — for the nightly labor begins and ends with torrents of black water, as a battle opens and concludes with black powder."

Germany

Germany followed its neighboring countries into coffee in the late 1600s. North Sea port cities of Hamburg and Bremen were first to see coffeehouses, and soon thereafter this newfangled beverage found its way to the rest of Germany.

Netherlands

Coffee was important as cargo before it caught on as a beverage in the Netherlands. And like what happened in other European countries, coffee took hold in the Netherlands by the late 1600s.

Perhaps even more significant was the Dutch success in acquiring live coffee trees in the early 1600s. In 1616, some seedlings were transported from the Yemeni Port of Mokha to the Botanical Gardens in Amsterdam. They thrived and were used by the Dutch 40 years later to help start coffee cultivation in Ceylon and southern India.

Coffee's ups and downs in England

By 1700 more than 2,000 coffeehouses were located in London. In each one the patrons often gathered because of their interests, occupations, religious affiliations, or politics.

Coffee had eclipsed beer and had gained a universality in England that was broadly enjoyed and praised by mostly men but few women. The environments for consumption weren't available to them, and they began to complain publicly. Petitions and proclamations against coffee were widespread.

Coffee's popularity in England waned in the 1700s. The penny universities evolved more and more into private and exclusive clubs, and new public tea gardens began to pop up. These tea emporiums were open to all, not exclusive to men. Tea brewing was far simpler than coffee preparation, and tea became more prevalent as England began its control over India and its significant export, tea.

Coffee and the American colonies

Across the sea the loyal British subjects of Boston enjoyed their first coffeehouse that opened in 1689. The separation between taverns and coffeehouses wasn't as clear in the New World, and patrons met to enjoy all types of beverages.

One such establishment was Boston's Green Dragon, a coffeehouse tavern operating from 1697 until 1832. At the Green Dragon famous rebellion leaders Paul Revere, John Adams, John Otis, and many others met to eventually plan their revolution.

When King George proposed the Stamp Act of 1765, those rebellion leaders were ready to respond with "No taxation without representation." Although the British government backed down on most of the proposed taxes, the tax on tea was to stay.

In 1773 with taxable British East India Tea Company tea exports flowing into the New World, the response was to dump it into the Boston Harbor. During the American Revolution tea drinking in the New World declined significantly, giving way to even more coffee drinking.

The Americas and first coffee trees

By the early 1700s coffee production was firmly entrenched in Africa and Indonesia. Coffee exporters brought names like Java, Mokha, Ethiopia, Kenya, and Sumatra to market. The Dutch were the most powerful of these importer/exporters and were the main traders to bring coffee to the Americas.

However, the Dutch weren't the only ones. Countries envious of the Dutch control dreamt of expanding their involvement in world travel and trade, and most realized that involvement in potential propagation was a significant step with clear long-term ambition. Hungry for opportunity, the French government was most grateful when the Dutch shared a healthy coffee plant with them.

The Dutch gifted a single and small specimen to Louis XIV. The coffee tree, known as the *noble tree,* began its arduous journey in Mokha, landed in Java, headed to Holland via ship, and then went by land to Paris where Louis XIV had orchestrated construction of the first greenhouse in Europe to house his specimen. This tree would yield seedlings after nine years in the Jardin des Plantes de Paris. A few of those seedlings would find their way into the hands of a somewhat crazed French naval officer, Gabriel Mathieu de Clieu.

He undertook what is recorded as an incredibly perilous journey. He protected his seedlings not only from the elements that included a most violent windy storm, but also from capture by another ship and a period of windless drifting when he rationed his own water in drops to keep the seedlings alive.

The seedlings flourished on Martinique, and it's believed that all the subsequent Typica plant stock found today in global coffee growth can be traced to those Typica variety initial plantings.

AN 18TH CENTURY TALE OF ROMANCE, INTRIGUE, DISPUTE, AND SMUGGLING

In 1727 French Guyana and Dutch Guyana (Suriname), located in the northeast of the continent of South America, a border dispute occurred, and the Guyanese governors engaged a Portuguese Brazilian neutral mediator to help them resolve the situation.

His name was Francisco de Melho Palheta. He agreed to serve them, knowing that he might also be able to use his involvement to gain access to some precious coffee seeds which neither government would allow to be exported.

While helping them sort out their business, he also began a clandestine romantic involvement with the French governor's wife. Upon successful completion of the government business his mistress presented him with a bouquet of flowers.

In the bouquet were coffee cherries that he planted back at his home in Para, a northern state of Brazil. The seeds he planted represented the first coffee planted in Brazil. Brazil is now the country with the largest coffee production (refer to Chapter 6 for more about Brazil's coffee industry).

Three centuries of dramatic change

The 18th, 19th, and early 20th centuries brought about dramatic social upheaval, multiple revolutions, world trade growth, and cultural and industrial developments moving at a faster pace than had ever been seen.

Increasingly, coffee was part of people's lives worldwide, from the intensely sought-after and rationed coffee and coffee chicory blend that was treasured by soldiers on both sides of the United States Civil War (refer to Figure 3-1) to multiple technological brewing advancements spawned as the Industrial Revolution opened up.

FIGURE 3-1: Civil War soldiers waiting in line for coffee.

Photo from Library of Congress

Inventions focused on improving the brewing and roasting methods. These included the siphon or vacuum brewer, the filter-style coffee brewer, espresso, large scale coffee roasting, canned, and instant coffee. (Chapters 11 and 12 discuss these different brewing and roasting methods in greater detail.)

As modern societies evolved, the quest for speed and simplicity sometimes eclipsed the ideas of craft and quality in the world of coffee. But this evolution wasn't singularly counter to craft and quality as it was that quest that brought the Italians to invent espresso, an entirely new and technologically sophisticated method for brewing that I detail in Chapter 12.

Chapter 4

Taking a Closer Look at Brewing Today

've lived through a tumultuous time as a coffee consumer during the past 50 years, and I've been asked many times not only what it was like, but also how it's connected to what you and I experience with coffee today.

This chapter dives into perhaps the most dramatic and relevant transition that has occurred in coffee history. Not only will you begin to see how the recognized grandfathers of the recently named specialty coffee industry came to recognize a huge opportunity, but you can also see its relevance to almost everything the coffee industry is going through and what people are experiencing when it comes to their coffee-drinking decisions today.

Understanding a Brewing Force — Alfred Peet and His Focus on Quality

The late 1960s saw coffee consumption in an interesting place. Even though breakfast coffee and the coffee break were firmly entrenched as societal norms, people were mostly drinking low-quality and harsh-tasting coffee.

Despite marketing promises of coffee tasting "heavenly" and "good to the last drop," coffee wasn't. A young visionary in Berkeley, California, was inspired to change that. The following sections describe how Alfred Peet, originally a native of the Netherlands, created specialty coffee and changed the coffee industry for good.

Buying, roasting, and creating a new coffee culture

After moving to the United States at the age of 35, Peet started working in the coffee-importing business. Driven by an acknowledgement and disappointment that coffee in the United States was of poor quality, he opened Peet's Coffee, Tea & Spices in 1966, 11 years after immigrating to this country.

REMEMBER

His small coffee shop soon expanded to three locations, and he established a reputation for uncompromisingly high quality in his first five years. Peet had learned roasting from his father, and at Peet's he carried on a tradition of dark roasting the beautiful green coffee he purchased. Through this roasting process, he felt that he could bring out the best qualities that coffee had to offer. When his customers eventually ground and brewed this coffee, they realized and enjoyed its full potential in the tasty results.

Generously growing the coffee community

Peet wasn't alone in his vision. Three young entrepreneurs in Seattle, Washington — Zev Siegl, Gordon Bowker, and Jerry Baldwin — and another in Cambridge, Massachusetts, George Howell, were all inspired by Peet's idea of making high-quality, fresh-roasted coffee available to consumers.

A sense of adventurous camaraderie must certainly have existed in those early days. The Starbucks founders — Siegl, Bowker, and Baldwin — had little knowledge of roasting when they started, but they each spent time with Peet in Berkeley, where he generously mentored them in the art of roasting.

Something big was brewing in both the Pacific Northwest and the Northeast, but for the moment these new coffee businesses — Peet's in Berkeley, Starbucks in Seattle, and the Coffee Connection in Cambridge, Massachusetts — were primarily focused on dry goods.

In the first Coffee Connection, located in what was an early shopping mall built in an old Harvard Square parking garage, guests accessed the second-floor shop by walking up the actual ramps used by cars prior to the remodel. Coffee was scooped from large barrels for take-away, and customers could sit and enjoy brewed coffee at either a small, low counter or at one of the few small tables. The coffee that was served was brewed in *cafetières,* also called French presses. Meanwhile, Peet's and Starbucks had no seats at all in their early establishments.

Specialty coffee is born

In 1974, in an issue of *Tea and Coffee Trade Journal*, Erna Knutsen, another of the early and respected pioneers of today's coffee industry (refer to Chapter 13 for more about her), was quoted as describing coffee she was buying and selling as *specialty coffee*. Her term described small quantities of coffee that were distinctly more complex and interesting than a great deal of what was being sold. She was among the first few coffee brokers to separate those coffee beans and offer them to the few small roasters who were beginning to build businesses around better-tasting coffee.

Equally as important, Peet realized consistency was key, because customers who bought one of his coffees might return in a week or two for a second purchase of what they had enjoyed. They'd expect that second drink to taste the same.

Giving customers something completely different than what they had experienced before was one thing. Opening their senses to what might be possible in the taste of a coffee was another. Pete built a business on those ideas.

Introducing Howard Schultz — the Father of Today's Starbucks

In 1982, a young housewares salesman named Howard Schultz traveled from New York to visit Starbucks, one of his accounts in Seattle. He was deeply moved by the ambience, the aromas, and the experience as he stepped into the small, wood-floored, dimly lit shop. He felt he had found his calling.

Not long thereafter, he moved to Seattle with his family and began working as the marketing head for this small Seattle coffee business. Little did he know that his move would mark the beginning of one of the world's specialty coffee juggernauts.

Traveling to Italy changed everything

In 1983, Schultz took a business trip to Italy, where he had another life-changing experience. While visiting Italian cafés, he tasted espresso and was struck by not only the beverage and its intensity, but also the baristas, their craft, and the dramatic atmosphere and palpable sense of community in the cafés.

He shared what he had seen and experienced with the Starbucks owners and his bosses. Although they were intrigued enough at first to support the opening of one Starbucks that would offer espresso beverages and seating, the idea didn't resonate with them. They really didn't want to be in the beverage business. They just didn't have the same passion that Schultz had, so in 1985 he left Starbucks to open Il Giornale, and by 1987 he had opened three stores in Seattle.

The original Starbucks owners had a change of heart and decided to offer Schultz a chance to purchase the company. He approached his investors, who had only recently helped fund the start of Il Giornale, and they once again took a risk by supporting his vision. Schultz purchased Starbucks and merged it with Il Giornale to form the start of the Starbucks the world knows today.

Expanding the business

Seventeen stores in Seattle and Vancouver became 33 in a year's time. By 1991 there were 116 stores, and Starbucks became the first privately owned U.S. company to offer a stock option program that even extended to part-time employees. By 1995 Starbucks had grown to more than 600 stores by first moving through the West Coast and then expanding east through Chicago and into Boston, New York, and Washington, D.C.

Starbucks wasn't the only specialty coffee company that was expanding. In 1984, Jerry Baldwin and a new investor group purchased Peet's, which had by then established dozens of stores in northern California. All three of the coffee trail-blazers (Peet's, Starbucks, and the Coffee Connection) had begun to firmly control the expansion of specialty coffee in the United States. In addition to Starbucks's rapid expansion, Peet's had dozens of West Coast stores, and the Coffee Connection had more than 20 locations in the New England area.

In 1995, Starbucks acquired the Coffee Connection, and by early 1996, the company had established international businesses in both Tokyo and Singapore. Perhaps more than any single coffee offering, Starbucks's Frappuccino launch in 1996 became a precursor to what the company offers today.

Expanding Brewed Specialty Coffee Worldwide

By 2002 a new cadre of passionate young coffee entrepreneurs in San Francisco, London, Melbourne, and Oslo, to just single out a few, began to emerge onto the global scene, beginning coffee businesses. These young men and women sensed an opportunity with coffee that could not only be personally rewarding but also offer financial rewards. They envisioned an approach that would deviate just enough from the successful businesses of the time like Starbucks and Peets to offer them a niche in which to operate. Their efforts established an emphasis on sourcing unique beans and brewing them for customers with a renewed sense of sharing stories about those coffees and their expertise in preparing them.

These sections consider a few individuals who took brewing coffee to the next level.

England breaks out

The scene in the United Kingdom is a respected one for coffee roasting and brewing, given some of the places and people. Shops like Monmouth Coffee with its unique coffee offerings, rustic feel, and multiple station hand-pouring brew bar have prevailed since 1978.

The following list, though by no means complete, highlights some important individuals in the UK coffee industry.

>> **Stephen Leighton:** Establishing Has Bean Coffee in 2000, Leighton, along with many of the new coffee scene purveyors, began to transition away from Peet's dark roast and full flavor, to a lighter roast, perceiving that the lighter roast was better able to highlight the coffee's subtleties and flavor nuances.

>> **Young Australian and New Zealand expatriates:** Several missing their home coffee scene opened shops such as Jo and Darren Howie's Sacred and Ian Burgess's Climpson and Sons. In 2005 Peter Hall, James Gurnsey, and Cameron McClure opened a legendary shop called Flat White in the London Soho neighborhood. Like many coffee shops at that time, they featured roasted beans from Monmouth.

>> **Gwilym Davies:** In 2016 he left Monmouth, opened a coffee cart, which led to additional coffee carts and eventually the opening of Prufrock Coffee. Davies won the 2009 World Barista Championship and has since assumed many collaborative consulting and teaching roles. His voice is influential voice in coffee today.

>> **James Hoffmann:** He's the training manager at La Spaziale UK and winner of the UK Barista Championship and later the World Barista Championship in 2007. Hoffmann and Anette Moldvaer, roaster and winner of the 2007 World Cup Tasters Championship, joined together to establish Square Mile Roasters in 2008.

U.S. brewers create excitement

San Francisco, Chicago, and Portland, Oregon, were becoming established as the hot spots for an influx of American coffee drinkers. Among them were Intelligentsia Coffee of Chicago, Stumptown of Portland, Counter Culture of Durham, North Carolina, and Wrecking Ball in San Francisco.

In fact, Trish Rothgeb (who cofounded Wrecking Ball with her husband Nick Cho) was credited with coining the term, *third wave*, that has come to define this global movement of transition in coffee. In 2003 she was quoted in an interview for the *Coffee Roasters Guild* newsletter. She described the waves as such:

>> **First wave:** The coffee industry began with an era or wave in which consumers simply drank coffee and didn't differentiate between where the bean came from or with types of beverages it made.

>> **Second wave:** Coffee moved into a second wave when Alfred Peet began to explore an artisanry around the roasting process and a focus on the origins of the beans he was roasting. Peets provided inspiration for another key business name from the second wave, Starbucks.

>> **Third wave:** Trish described an even more focused effort on the uniqueness of green coffee origins and how that uniqueness may be shared with consumers. What made third wavers stand out was they also were discussing a roasting philosophy that emphasized exploring and revealing the nuances of flavor.

Meeting consumer demands

The past ten-plus years have represented an unprecedented proliferation of coffee opportunities for consumers. Large coffee companies have opened at a mind-blowing pace and thousands of small cafés have opened at the same time.

The consumer base has grown, and those consumers, both established and new adopters, demand even broader opportunities for access, technologically consistent transaction enhancements, and innovative efficiencies. Things like drive-through, online shopping, delivery, and mobile order and pay gained popularity.

Consumer demand for modern convenience in coffee, which was first seen in the growth and adoption of instant coffee in the 1940s and 1950s, now drives the development of new and unique form factors like pods or capsules for brewing. Keurig's Green Mountain Coffee and Nestlé's Nespresso single-cup brewing systems, while seen at first as lower in quality and gimmicky, have captured an increasing percentage of coffee consumers, and many of the brands I highlight in this chapter as being instrumental in creating the specialty coffee industry are now collaborating to ensure that their coffees and roasting craft are featured as part of that single-cup brewing trend.

Understanding the Role of the National Coffee Association

As a passionate coffee consumer I've always been interested in the trends happening in the coffee business, and I turn to some of the best data available, which comes from the National Coffee Association (NCA), a leading U.S.-based trade association that conducts the most comprehensive market research into what consumers are doing when coffee buying and brewing.

The NCA shared these highlights in its 2020 annual overview.

Overall coffee consumption

A lot of coffee brewing — at home, by take-out, or in a business — is happening every day. Consider these stats:

» Sixty-two percent of Americans drink coffee daily.

» Past-day consumption of coffee (meaning the number of people surveyed who reported drinking coffee within the past day) has risen by 5 percent since 2015.

» Seven in ten Americans drink coffee at least once per week.

» Fifty-three percent of coffee drinkers want to buy coffee that is good for the environment, for coffee farmers, and for communities whereas 47 percent apparently don't care.

» Nearly half of daily coffee drinkers who buy coffee outside their home purchase it at a drive-through.

» Twenty-five percent of people ordering coffee outside their home within the past week did so through an app.

Coffee drink trends

As consumers get out there and enjoy their brew or make their coffee at home, what are they consuming? This list highlights the choices:

» Consumption of *gourmet coffee* (defined merely as "brewed from premium beans") is up 25 percent since 2015, although it didn't increase over 2019's level. (Specialty coffee is sometimes referred to as gourmet coffee.)

» Twenty percent of Americans take their coffee black.

>> Consumption of espresso-based beverages continues to increase. The most popular espresso-based beverages (in order of percentage of people who drank one within the past year) were as follows:

- Cappuccino (33 percent)
- Latte (33 percent)
- Frozen blended (28 percent)
- Espresso (26 percent)
- Mocha (23 percent)
- Macchiato (18 percent)
- Americano (18 percent)
- Flat white (8 percent)

Chapter 12 explains what ingredients go in these drinks.

>> Home-brewing equipment has changed dramatically over the past five years, with Americans now 24 percent less likely to use a traditional drip coffee machine than they were in 2015. Meanwhile, ownership of single-cup brewers is up 50 percent over the past five years.

>> Four percent of drinkers reported using alternative milks daily.

>> Forty percent of Americans add some kind of milk and sweetener.

>> The number of Americans adding only milk but no sweetener has increased by 66 percent since 2015.

Coffee drinking by generation

This list highlights the generational differences and offers a glimpse at the direction coffee businesses might go as they look to charting the future of coffee consumers:

>> Coffee drinkers aged 60 and older are more than twice as likely to consume traditional, non-gourmet coffee than 18- to 24-year-olds.

>> Drinkers aged 25 to 39 led the increase in espresso-based beverages, which are favored by 27.5 percent of Americans younger than 40, compared to 17 percent for seniors.

>> Nine out of ten older coffee drinkers have coffee at breakfast, compared to seven out of ten of the youngest drinkers, who are almost twice as likely to drink coffee at lunchtime as their older counterparts.

>> Coffee consumption increases with age, although since 2015, consumption is up 40 percent among drinkers aged 18 to 24, and nearly 25 percent for drinkers aged 25 to 39.

3

Taking a Trip around the World

Understand what sourcing means for coffee and how it plays an essential role in the cup or cups you drink every morning.

Find out where coffee grows — the Coffee Belt — and comprehend what makes that geographic region so unique.

Take a deeper dive into coffee-growing regions and coffee-growing countries and begin to grasp some of the links to geography and flavor.

Read about the familiar origins of coffee and also some unfamiliar ones that may surprise you.

Chapter **5**

Sourcing Coffee — Digging In to Where Coffee Comes From

E ven as a new coffee drinker many cups ago I understood that coffee was coming from someplace distant. Country names I associated mostly with Central and Latin America popped up frequently as part of coffee marketing, and other names like Sumatra or Papua New Guinea made appearances and contributed to coffee's mystique and reminded me of my youthful ignorance when it came to world geography.

This chapter offers you something I'd have thoroughly appreciated in my early days of exploring coffee — an introduction into the geography of coffee (where it's grown and produced) and a focus on some of the important natural elements influencing coffee growing.

Taking a Bird's-Eye Look: The Coffee Belt

Chapter 3 identifies the Coffee Belt, an area near the equator where coffee is grown today. The equator defines the middle of the earth, and on that circumference between the Tropics of Cancer and Capricorn you can get a better idea that brings the world its coffee. Figure 5-1 identifies the countries where coffee is grown and produced around the world today.

Here I dive deeper into the top coffee-producing countries and discuss what makes these countries prime for coffee production.

Identifying the top coffee producers

Look at Figure 5-1 to identify where the following 50 coffee-producing countries are. The first 25 listed here are the world's top producers. I place an asterisk beside the top Arabica producers (although these countries aren't listed in order or Arabica production):

>> Brazil *

>> Vietnam *

>> Colombia *

>> Indonesia *

>> Ethiopia *

>> Honduras *

>> India *

>> Mexico *

>> Peru *

>> Uganda

>> Guatemala *

>> Nicaragua *

>> China *

>> Malaysia

>> Ivory Coast

>> Costa Rica *

>> Tanzania

>> Papua New Guinea *

>> Thailand

>> El Salvador

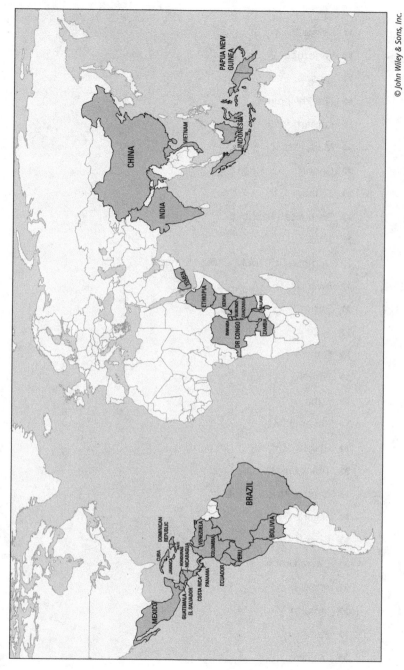

© John Wiley & Sons, Inc.

FIGURE 5-1:
The Coffee
Belt today.

- » Kenya *
- » Venezuela
- » Laos
- » The Philippines
- » Cameroon
- » Madagascar
- » Gabon
- » Ecuador
- » Dominican Republic
- » Haiti
- » Democratic Republic of the Congo
- » Rwanda
- » Burundi
- » Togo
- » Guinea
- » Yemen
- » Cuba
- » Panama
- » Bolivia
- » Timor-Leste
- » Central African Republic
- » Nigeria
- » Ghana
- » Sierra Leone
- » Angola
- » Jamaica
- » Paraguay
- » Malawi
- » Trinidad and Tobago
- » Zimbabwe

Chapters 6, 7, and 8 dive deeper into the geography of coffee and focus on many of the top coffee-producing countries. I discuss some historical and political factors that affected coffee production and examine flavor profiles and methods of processing.

Recognizing what makes these countries so unique to growing coffee

A closer look at these coffee-producing countries reveals why geography is so important. In order for coffee to grow, the coffee farms in these countries need to be located where the following factors are present.

Elevation

Elevation is an extremely important element. The ideal elevation is 3,000–6,000 feet (900–1,900 meters). If Figure 5-1 were topographic, it would reveal a correlation between the areas where coffee is most abundant and areas of more mountainous terrain.

REMEMBER

The reason elevation is a key factor has to do with the slower growth that coolness at higher altitudes promotes. The coffee's slower maturation allows for complex sugars to develop, and the bean develops an increased density.

Elevation factors into the tastes of Arabica no matter where you find coffee, and the following list explains how taste can change with elevation and top producers:

>> **Very high altitude (1,500 meters/5,000 ft):** These coffees are fruity, spicy floral, berry, and complex. You can find this Arabica in Ethiopia, Colombia, Kenya, Guatemala, Sulawesi, and Papua New Guinea.

>> **High altitude (1,200 meters/4,000 ft):** These coffees' taste descriptors include citrus, vanilla, chocolate, nutty, and complex. You can find this Arabica in Costa Rica, Java, Sumatra, Nicaragua, and Mexico.

>> **Medium altitude (900 meters/3,000 ft):** These coffees are smooth, sweet, and less complex. You can find them in Brazil.

>> **Low altitude (760 meters/2,500 ft):** These coffees are subtle, soft, mild, simple, and less complex. You can find them in Hawaii.

Volcanic soil

Volcanic soil is known for its rich and abundant nutrients and for its capacity to hold moisture because of its ash content. So, the dirt is essential to growing coffee.

REMEMBER

Coffee growers face an ongoing environmental struggle. Mountain terrain is subject to erosion and soil washout (see Figure 5-2), so growers must sometimes take steps to fortify the dirt around individual trees on a hillside. Specifically, they might work the dirt around the base of a tree or even dig drainage and pooling areas to move or control water in a deluge.

FIGURE 5-2: Erosion and soil washout is a serious problem for coffee growers.

Photo by Major Cohen

Understanding Nature's Role in Growing Coffee

All agricultural products are at the mercy of whatever Mother Nature delivers, and sustained success really depends on some predictability and consistency. Today all farms and their products are experiencing challenges to both, and to say that growers are learning as they go is realistic and a bit disconcerting.

Unfortunately Mother Nature is unpredictable. The following weather conditions can significantly affect the coffee harvest:

>> **Moisture:** Moisture is crucial, delivered in the form of rain, often during a specific rainy season, which to the grower is part of the cyclical, annual growing season. However, rain can sometimes come in downpours, and other times growers experience drought.

The ideal rainfall amount for Arabica growth is between 60 to 100 inches (1,500 and 2,500 mm) of rain, which will fall over about nine months while the coffee is growing.

>> **Temperature:** Coffee grows in locations on or near the equator. Within the growing band, the temperatures are high, typically ranging from 59 to 75° F (15 to 24°C). Nature delivers, and growers pray for predictability and consistency with temperatures.

>> **Wind:** Wind can have tremendous impact. At any point in the year excessive wind can impact the trees as they stand, relatively unprotected on the mountainside.

WARNING

Winds during the brief, three- or four-day period in the annual coffee growing cycle when the trees are in flower can especially be dangerous.

If those precious and fragrant flowers, which normally only last on the branch for a few days, are blown off before they've reached their full potential, then more than likely the coffee fruit, the cherry, won't form, resulting in a reduced harvest.

Recognizing How Climate Change Is Changing Coffee

I've probably fielded more questions regarding the impact of climate change on coffee in the past few years than on any other topic. Two specific climate-related factors are impacting the coffee industry today:

>> **An increase in airborne fungus:** Leaf rust (*Hemileia vastatrix*) destroys the coffee tree leaf, thus ending any chance the tree has to grow and produce fruit. The fungus first appears as small, pale yellow spots on the top of coffee leaves. It eventually spreads until the infected leaf falls off, leaving a bare branch. Leaf rust can affect most types of Arabica coffee.

>> **Changes in the weather pattern:** Changes in the weather, such as a rise in annual temperatures at certain elevations and the development and strength of storms, are significantly affecting coffee.

ON THE WEB

The World Coffee Research (www.worldcoffeeresearch.org) is perhaps the most well-known organization doing work to ensure that coffee farmers' livelihoods and the businesses that depend on those farmers address the threats of climate change. One recent study looked at areas where coffee grows today and forecast that by 2050 half of the land will be unsuitable for Arabica production as a direct result of climate change. The group's work is extensive. Check out the website if you're interested in staying up-to-date with current developments with the connection between climate and coffee.

ON THE WEB

Starbucks and Nestlé, two of the biggest coffee companies in the world, have taken positions in addressing environmental and other issues threatening coffee's future. Using their size and influence for good, their efforts are noble and transparently open to review at www.starbucks.com/responsibility/sourcing and https://courses.starbucksglobalacademy.com/courses. Check out www.nestlecoffeepartnerssl.com for more about what Nestlé is doing. Several other coffee companies, large and small, are also addressing threats to coffee sustainability. You can also follow the National Coffee Association's effort at www.ncausa.org/sustainability.

ASSESSING A COFFEE FARM: HOW WELL IS IT RUNNING?

I've visited many coffee farms through my career. People often ask me most about the majesty or beauty of the farms. They ask me less about the farm's specific elements that relate to the lives of the farmer and the farmer's family that relate to producing high quality coffee on a consistent basis.

Imagine you're headed to a coffee farm. Picture you've been asked to assess the work going on at this farm during your visit, perhaps as a coffee buyer.

Perhaps it's a small, self-enclosed, fully integrated operation. That is, it has trees mature enough to cherry, a nursery for growing new seedlings, a small processing machine, and an area for drying. Perhaps it's an even smaller farm, maybe a member of a cooperative where the mill for processing is a separate facility some distance away. Or, perhaps it's an even larger fully integrated operation with significant acreage, a factory-like processing mill, and numerous drying patios or mechanical dryers.

No matter the size of the farm, focus on these priority areas during your assessment:

- **Economics:** *Economics* is important because you want to ensure that the people doing the work are receiving a fair wage. Determine whether they're being paid fairly for their work, they're being paid in a timely manner, and that financial records are being kept that document those transactions.

- **Social responsibility:** *Social responsibility* is focusing on the lives of the people doing the work and their families. Socially responsible practices associated to financial transparency include some freedom of communication and perhaps even collective bargaining among the workers. Hours being worked, use of children as laborers, nondiscrimination practices, housing, and access to water and sanitary facilities all should be on your list of considerations. Access to education, medical care and training, and safety also deserve inclusion in this part of your assessment.

- **Environment:** *Environmental factors* are important to assess because good practices ensure sustainability, and bad practices doom it and the future capacity to grow coffee there. Look out for the following in your assessment:

  - **Water body protection and maintenance of buffer zones surrounding that water:** Make sure existing bodies of water are protected to ensure pollutants or debris aren't compromising them and ensure the farm is maintaining buffer zones of shore and foliage to ensure wildlife habitat is protected.

  - **The farm's water usage and irrigation practices:** Water is a precious resource; without water, the farm couldn't grow coffee.

  - **Control of surface erosion control and soil quality:** Physical fortification diminishes rainfall soil runoff; soil is regularly analyzed to stay apprised of its makeup.

  - **Use of shade trees to create canopy:** Controlling the temperature and considering the wildlife that reside or rest under the canopy are also important.

  - **Use of an ecological pest and disease control plan:** The coffee trees interact with different insects. Some are beneficial like the bees moving among the trees in their quest for flowers. Some can create issues like coffee borer beetle, which bores its way right through ripe cherry, destroying the bean inside. Look for this plan that integrated pest management (IPM) outlines. The World Health Organization (WHO) has provided well-researched, impactful guidance on farms using control substances that balance an effective control with long-term productivity.

  - **Responses to climate change:** Look for evidence of minimizing water consumption and reducing wastewater impacts. Actual waste management, including the handling of wet parchment, dry hull, and even chopped wood from tree renewal, is also important to investigate.

Chapter 6

Considering the Western Hemisphere

What better place to start a tour of the Coffee Belt than in the Americas, which includes Central and South Americas, the Caribbean, and Hawaii. This chapter includes some of the most familiar country names, and more than likely you've drank coffee from one of these locations. Knowing more about their history, processing practices, and general taste characteristics in the cup can help you make choices. Although I've personally liked several coffees from these locations, my all-time favorite is Guatemala.

REMEMBER

Central America includes countries that connect North and South America and are located between Mexico and Colombia. Latin America is a much broader term and includes Central America as well as Mexico and all the countries of South America. The seven countries that comprise Central America are Guatemala, Belize, El Salvador, Honduras, Nicaragua, Costa Rica, and Panama.

Another valuable clarification I need to make here addresses two of my favorite origins: Jamaica and Hawaii. I include them because of their physical proximity and the similarity of important factors related to geography, weather, soil, elevation, and so on, all of which impact coffee cultivation. Hawaii is the only state in the United States that grows coffee.

Figure 6-1 illustrates where coffee is grown in the Americas and the Caribbean.

FIGURE 6-1:
The Americas.

© *John Wiley & Sons, Inc.*

Eyeing Central America's Influence on Coffee Production

One thing is clear about Central American coffee: The range of coffee flavors that these countries deliver is astonishing, with remarkable descriptions like intense sweetness, bright acidity, juicy fruitiness, chocolatey richness, and nutty being just a few. Here is a closer look at these coffee juggernauts.

Costa Rica

Coffee has been grown in Costa Rica since 1779. With a significant amount of ideal volcanic, mountainous terrain, and a superb climate for coffee production, coffee flourished, and it took only 50 years for coffee export to eclipse formerly dominant trade exports of cacao, tobacco, and sugar.

The best known regional names to watch for include the following:

>> The West Central Valley where Naranjo is often highlighted

>> The Los Santos region where Terrazu coffees are grown

>> The East Central Valley, Tres Rios region, where two distinct seasons and the Irazu volcanic soil result in noteworthy coffees from this small area

All three regions (see Figure 6-2) have established long-standing reputations for extremely consistent, high-quality coffees featuring superb acidity, body, and flavor.

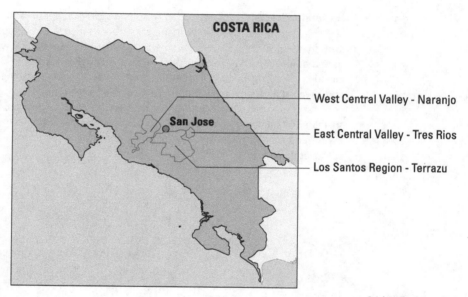

FIGURE 6-2: Coffee-growing regions in Costa Rica.

Coffee's history in Costa Rica surpasses 200 years. During that time, washed coffee processing has been the go-to method, which necessitates using a lot of clean water and can create compromised wastewater at the end. (See Chapter 2 for detailed info about washed coffee processing and other processing methods.)

REMEMBER

Costa Rica is a leader in environmentally sustainable coffee production. The increasing number of small wet mills doing washed coffee processing and fully integrated (end-to-end involving growing, picking, processing, drying, and bagging) processing along with mandated government oversight of water usage and water waste has given Costa Rica the edge over many of the world's coffee producers seeking sustainability.

VISIT A COFFEE FARM

Costa Rica is recognized as one of the world's greatest tourist locations for ecotourism and tropical exploration. Along with spectacular coastal destinations, it's one of the few places where visiting a working coffee farm is possible. Two of the most dramatic locations aren't far from San José in the Central Valley:

- **Doka Estate Coffee Tour** (www.dokaestate.com), hosted at the Vargas family farm that has been in existence since 1940, is celebrated for the historical perspective and up-close immersion it offers. You can spend time in the coffee fields and see firsthand the movement of coffee from those fields into a complex wet mill and finally onto the drying patios.

- **Hacienda Alsacia,** Starbucks Coffee Farm and Visitor Center (www.starbuckscoffeefarm.com), offers a dramatic, comprehensive micro-mill tour of the only farm that Starbucks owns. Nestled on the mountainside part of the way up the road that leads to Poas Volcano, this spectacularly striking group of buildings includes a working mill and a unique café with a deck overlooking the Central Valley and a waterfall. Well-versed tour guides host the coffee tours and a talented cadre of baristas man the café. Most noteworthy here is the opportunity to explore the sustainability initiatives because it's also home to the Starbucks Farmer Support Center and Agronomy offices. The following photo gives you an idea of the beauty at Hacienda Alsacia.

Photo by Major Cohen

Sweet, clean, sometimes a bit nutty are often description terms used for Costa Rican coffees.

El Salvador

Coffee production in El Salvador began in the 1850s. As the government supported the growth of the industry, El Salvador was the world's fourth largest producer by 1880 with three predominant growing regions: Apaneca–Ilamatepec to the west, Altotepec which is central, and Tecapa–Chinameca to the east.

Unfortunately the 1980 civil war rocked roughly 100 years of stability in production and dramatically impacted the country's coffee-growing business. This strife also impacted technological development, somewhat indirectly preventing the changes being made by many El Salvador producers to plant high yield varieties as opposed to the heirloom varieties all had been supporting for many years.

As a result, consumers today are the beneficiaries because producers, both large and small, are delivering coffees from heirloom El Salvador production that are incredibly complex, super sweet, and quite tasty. The Apaneca-Ilamatepec region (see Figure 6-3) continues to be a steady coffee-producing region.

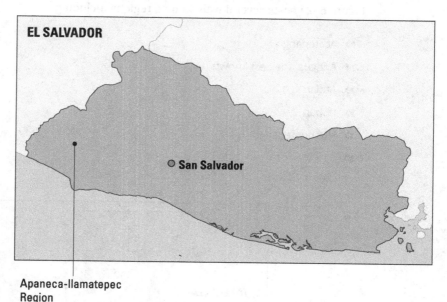

EL SALVADOR

San Salvador

Apaneca-Ilamatepec
Region

FIGURE 6-3:
The Apaneca-Ilamatepec region in El Salvador.

© John Wiley & Sons, Inc.

Washed processing is the predominant method used in El Salvador, although, like its neighboring coffee-producing countries, there is experimentation going on constantly. See Chapter 2 for more information about processing.

ON THE WEB

Highlighting an amazing coffee farm for you here. Carlos and Julie Batres are renowned, fifth-generation stewards of Montecarlos, a prized coffee estate in Apaneca. The beautiful farm is situated on a volcano that provides rich soil and dynamic topography for growing world class coffees. Montecarlos (www. montecarlosestate.com) was the first estate in the world to develop and plant the Pacamara coffee variety.

Guatemala

An amazing diversity of climate and culture makes Guatemala unique among its neighboring countries. Coffee production can be traced to the 1750s but didn't really begin to gain importance as a cash crop until the mid-1800s.

Periodic government instability and internal turmoil impacted production throughout the 1900s. Despite those issues Guatemala rose into the top ten coffee producers in the world and holds a place there today.

Mountainous volcanic terrain across the southern third of Guatemala (refer to Figure 6-4) hosts several well-known regions including

>> Acatenango

>> Antigua, the best known

>> Atitlan

>> Cobán

>> Huehuetenango

>> San Marcos

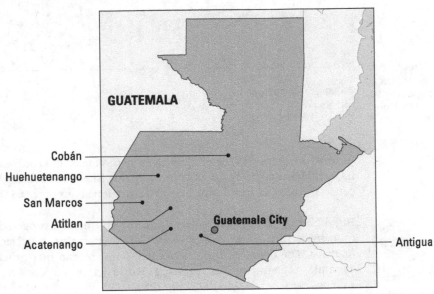

FIGURE 6-4: Coffee-growing regions in Guatemala.

© John Wiley & Sons, Inc.

Harvesting begins in December and can last until March. Washed processing of cherry is the most common method used. Refer to Chapter 2 for more details about processing.

Coffees from Guatemala are known for their diversity of taste profiles. They're often described broadly as elegant and more specifically as chocolatey, nutty, sweet, cocoa-like as well as bright, rich, creamy, and complex. Guatemalan coffees are often the coffees that exhibit a balance of acidity and body where neither quality is predominant, which when coupled with some of the flavor notes make them a favorite choice of many.

Honduras

The recent success of Honduran coffee producers has been noteworthy given the late start the country had because it really only began significant production in the early 1800s, much later than its neighboring Central American countries.

Today Honduras is among the leading Central American coffee-producing countries. More and more growers and processors are recognizing the advantages possible if they bring higher quality production to the market.

Notable growing regions (see Figure 6-5) across the mountainous central and southern part of the country are

>> Agalta

>> Comayagua

>> Copán

>> Montecillos

>> Opalca

>> El Paraíso

Honduran coffees have a wide variety of taste profile characteristics; among the most memorable are varied levels of fruitiness and pronounced acidity. Washed processing and drying incorporating both sun and mechanical dryer are most commonly used.

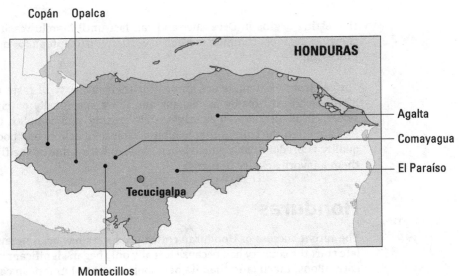

Copán Opalca

HONDURAS

Agalta

Comayagua

El Paraíso

Tecucigalpa

Montecillos

FIGURE 6-5:
Coffee-growing
areas in
Honduras.

© John Wiley & Sons, Inc.

Mexico

Coffee growing began in Mexico in the late 1700s, but it wasn't until the 1920s and the end of the Mexican Revolution that production began in earnest. Infrastructure development and the establishment of the Mexican Coffee Institute in 1973 set the stage for advancement, but political turmoil stifled real progress.

Small collectives of growers dominate the business in Mexico today. Although the country isn't a significant large producer, many coffees being exported from Mexico receive high praise for their quality and consistency.

Three Mexican states (refer to Figure 6-6) most known for their coffee output are

» Chiapas

» Oaxaca

» Veracruz

Washed coffee processing dominates in Mexico, and the output is known for incredible diversity. Mexican coffees exhibit a wonderfully wide range of taste characteristics from delicate, light bodied, and sweet to sometimes more earthy and a bit spicy.

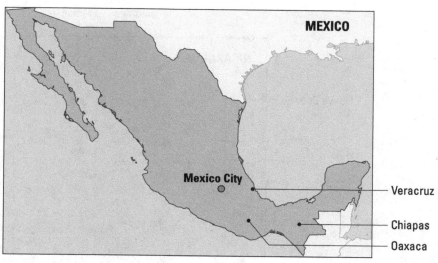

MEXICO

Mexico City

Veracruz

Chiapas

Oaxaca

FIGURE 6-6:
Coffee-growing
regions in Mexico.

© John Wiley & Sons, Inc.

Nicaragua

Coffee growing began in Nicaragua in 1790 but didn't become a significant revenue-producing agricultural export until the 1840s. In the more than a century since then, Nicaragua coffee production has become crucial to the country's economy to the point that coffee is now Nicaragua's primary export. More than 200,000 jobs and more than 40,000 farmers depend on coffee for their livelihoods.

Consistent with neighboring countries in Latin America, Nicaragua's industry and infrastructure is hampered by decades of political unrest and instability, civil wars, and natural disasters.

Washed coffee processing dominates in the key coffee-growing regions (see Figure 6-7) whose departments and cities include

>> Estelí

>> Jinotega

>> Madriz

>> Matagalpa

>> Nueva Segovia

Nicaraguan coffees deliver a wide range in tastes from sweetness and complexity to mild acidity and fruitiness. The past decade has seen considerable increase in quality in offerings from Nicaragua.

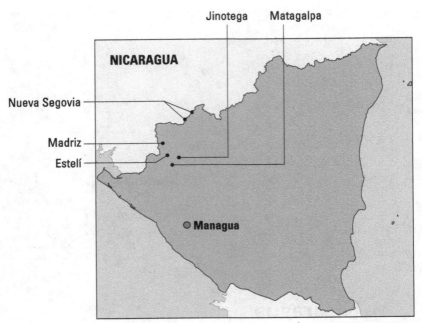

Jinotega   Matagalpa

NICARAGUA

Nueva Segovia

Madriz

Estelí

○ Managua

FIGURE 6-7:
Coffee-growing
regions in
Nicaragua.

© John Wiley & Sons, Inc.

Panama

European immigrants brought coffee to Panama when they settled in the late 19th century. Despite its location between two respected exporting countries — Costa Rica to the west and north and Colombia to the south and east — compared to its neighbors, Panama isn't a significant producer of any quantities of coffee.

The most well-known growing regions in Panama (refer to Figure 6-8) are

>> Boquete in Chiriqui

>> Renacimiento

>> Volcán in Chiriqui

Coffees from Panama are processed predominantly using the washed process method, Geishas included. The coffee is commonly described as light, pleasant, sweet, and a bit floral or citrusy. First-time tasters, like the judges in that Panamanian competition of 2005, were often struck with a sense of never having tasted such delicious coffee.

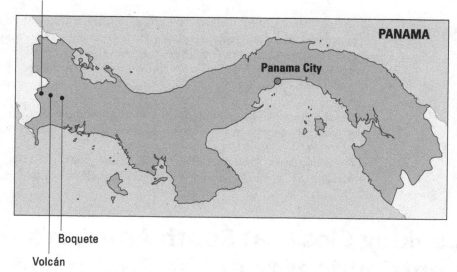

FIGURE 6-8:
Coffee-growing
regions in
Panama.

© John Wiley & Sons, Inc.

ON THE WEB

A BLAST FROM THE PAST REIGNITES PANAMA'S COFFEE INDUSTRY

A rediscovery of an almost lost Arabica variety, Geisha, in the early 2000s, led to a resurgence of this coffee, a change in overall perception of Panama as a growing region, and a global reverberation that still resonates today.

The Geisha varietal originated in Ethiopia and came to Panama in the 1960s as part of efforts to find coffee varietals with resistance to an airborne enemy, leaf rust. Although the plants had that quality, they also suffered from brittle branches and lower production, so farmers weren't fans. A few carried on and mixes of multiple varieties were the outcome.

In 2005 the Peterson family, who owned Hacienda La Esmeralda (https://haciendaesmeralda.com), kept their Geisha separated and entered it in the Specialty Coffee Association of Panama's "Best of Panama" competition. It won the competition and broke all records at the subsequent auction, garnering a price of $20 per pound green.

(continued)

(continued)

The news of the Geisha from Esmeralda spread rapidly around the world and in the following years Geisha coffees have begun to find favor among some of the world's most renowned coffee producers. Additionally, the coffees have become dominant on the world stages where coffee competitors have been serving Geisha's varietals from different countries to the judges.

Of course, not all Geisha coffee crops are noteworthy, because without careful growing and processing conditions, the coffee can be lower quality and have bad taste.

Described as sweet, floral, and citrusy, the Geisha taste profile exhibits an unmatched clarity and complexity when nature and processing methodology are in alignment.

Looking Closer at South America's Contributions to Coffee Production

With the world's top coffee producer Brazil and perhaps the best-known Colombia topping the list of South America coffee sources, this area maintains an incredibly important influence in the global coffee world.

The entire world market is impacted by crop success or failure in Brazil and forecasts detailing crop output and weather can affect prices everywhere. Offsetting the behemoth Brazil are some smaller but noteworthy producing countries worth exploring.

Bolivia

Although Bolivia isn't one of the world's largest coffee producers, this central South American country has a long history of producing coffee throughout the 19th and 20th centuries.

Even though coffee producers in the late 1800s until the late 20th century often saw their efforts compromised by dramatic temperature swings that negatively impacted quality coffee production during processing, in the past 20 years coffee producers in Bolivia have established a reputation for some small amounts of significantly special tasting coffees.

One area known for coffee production in Bolivia is Yungas (see Figure 6-9), an area recognized for high quality, delicious coffees.

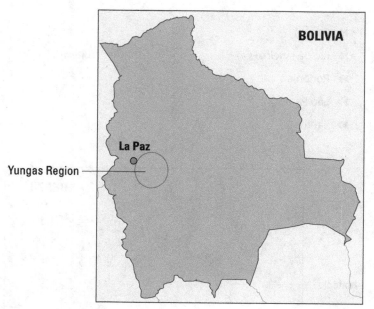

FIGURE 6-9:
The Yungas
region in Bolivia.

Bolivian coffees primarily use washed processing, and growing occurs at 2,600 to 7,500 feet above sea level. Tastes vary considerably, but often highlight bright acidity, delicate sweetness, and fruit notes like lemon, pear, apple, and apricot.

Brazil

Coffee didn't arrive in Brazil as a crop until 1727. Despite not being a native plant, coffee production has flourished there, and Brazil is now the top ranked producer in the world. Production levels in the early 1800s established Brazil's dominance, accounting for more 30 percent of the world's entire production.

By the early 1900s Brazil was responsible for more than 80 percent of the world's coffee production, but greater production elsewhere in the world has reduced Brazil's coffee production to around 30 percent, although the country is still the world's top producer.

Brazil's largest coffee growing state responsible for more than 50 percent of the country's coffee is Mina Gerais. Other states include (see Figure 6-10)

>> Bahia

>> Espirito Santo

- » Paraná
- » Rio de Janeiro
- » Rodônia
- » Sâo Paulo
- » Santo

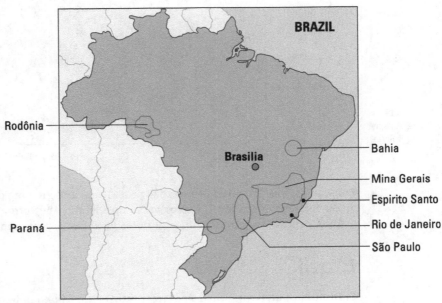

FIGURE 6-10:
Coffee-growing
regions in Brazil.

© John Wiley & Sons, Inc.

More producers in Brazil use natural processing than any other method, although industrious, increasingly more world-savvy growers are exploring multiple processing methods to create a diversity of flavors in the hopes of greater revenue return for their coffees among increasingly sophisticated buyers and consumers. Washed (wet), pulped natural (semi-washed), and dry (natural) Arabicas are produced as well as a fair amount of Robusta. Refer to Chapter 2 for more details about the different ways that coffee is produced.

Brazil has the most technologically advanced methods for production in the world today. These include mechanical harvesting and advanced infrastructure that support coffee at every step of its journey from cherry to bean. With a clear prioritization of production speed and high yields over the last 150 years, a reputation of somewhat lower quality was established. However, recent efforts by many producers have begun to result in some splendid, high quality, delicious Brazilian coffees.

With all processing methods being used in Brazil the coffees have an incredible variety of taste potential. In general, and at their best they're considered sweet, with caramel and chocolate notes, pronounced body, and low acidity.

Colombia

When you think of South American coffee, more than likely Colombia comes to mind. And you'd be accurate. Colombia (not Columbia — a common misspelling) has a long history for coffee production that spans the past 300 years. That history coupled with some significantly powerful marketing has established Colombia as the first country named when people are surveyed, "Name a country that produces coffee."

The National Federation of Coffee Growers of Colombia put together a time-tested and successful marketing strategy that included the invented character Juan Valdez, the slogan "mountain grown coffee," and the promise of "100 percent Colombian coffee." Colombia's coffee producers are responsible for growing and exporting some of the most noteworthy Arabica coffees in the world market.

Washed coffee processing is the most widely utilized method for green coffee production. Although elevation is significant and consistent across all the Colombia growing regions, some noteworthy taste characteristics have come to be associated with certain of the regions. Some of the most notable areas shown in Figure 6-11 include

>> **Nariño region:** Known for coffees that exhibit stunning juicy acidity, nutty, and cocoa flavors as well as marked complexity

>> **Santander region:** Found to be rounder and sweeter

Ecuador

Coffee production in Ecuador started in 1860, much later than many other South America countries. Both Arabica and Robusta varieties are grown there, with the country's production at about 60 percent Arabica and 40 percent Robusta.

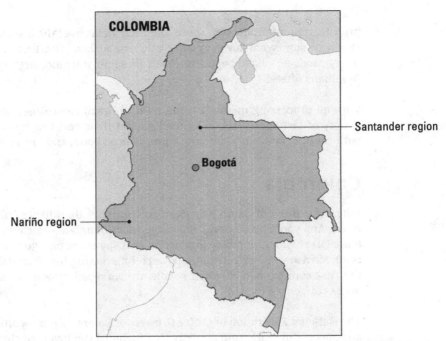

FIGURE 6-11:
Coffee-growing regions in Colombia.

Ecuador is ranked 20th in world production, far behind neighbors Brazil (No. 1), Colombia (No. 3), and Peru (No. 11).

Coffee production in Ecuador is in the hands of growers with small farms of 1 to 10 hectares. Notable Ecuadorian coffee-producing provinces shown in Figure 6-12 include

- » Azuay
- » Carchi
- » Chimborazo
- » Imbabura
- » Loja
- » El Oro
- » Pichincha
- » Tungurahua
- » Zamora-Chinchipe

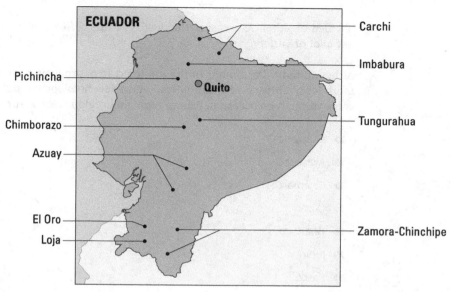

FIGURE 6-12:
Coffee-growing
regions in
Ecuador.

Coffee growers generally use natural or sun-dried processing (refer to Chapter 2 for the different processing methods). In the past decade coffee aficionados have started noticing some Ecuadorian coffees as specialty coffee standouts. Most of the past coffee production has been made into soluble or instant coffees.

Arabica production today has been described as creamy with intense sweetness, pronounced acidity, and flavors reminiscent of stone fruits like peaches and plums.

REMEMBER

Keep an eye on Ecuador. Its climate and geography make the country poised for greatness should anyone decide to invest in developing a more robust business there.

Peru

Coffee started in Peru high in the Andes Mountains sometime in the late 1700s. Although the production capacity grew in the next 100 years, the coffee grown was consumed domestically. Not until 1887 did significant exports to Europe from Peru begin. Government turmoil and extremely limited infrastructure investment plagued Peru's coffee industry until the 1980s when nongovernment organizations like Fair Trade identified an increasing interest in Peru as a potential and powerful source of coffee.

What's unique to Peru's coffee production is the importance of cooperative growing arrangements that make up a significant number of the producers in Peru. Coffee coming from cooperatives is collected from individual farm members and blended together. As a result, the quality of this coffee is often quite similar with not a lot of variety.

Although today Peru ranks in the top ten coffee-producing countries, it's known more for quantity over quality. However, a few noteworthy individual export lots come through on occasion. Primary growing regions (see Figure 6-13) are

>> Amazonas

>> Ayacucho

>> Cajamarca

>> Cusco

>> Huanaco

>> Junín

>> Pasco

>> Puno

>> San Martín

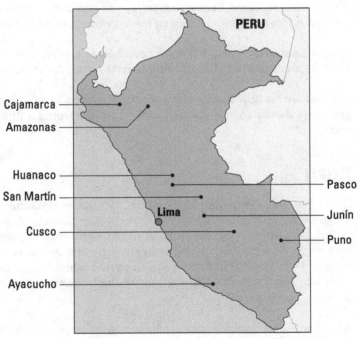

FIGURE 6-13:
Coffee-growing
regions in Peru.

© John Wiley & Sons, Inc.

FOCUSING ON THE FAIR IN FAIR TRADE AND OTHER CERTIFICATIONS

At its simplest Fair Trade is a way for producers in developing countries to realize sustainable and equitable trade relationships. That is, they can receive a fair price for their work. Effective marketing of the Fair Trade program since its start in the 1970s has made it a familiar and often mentioned way for consumers to support origin workers and their families and feel good about their purchase as a result.

In addition to Fair Trade Certification, numerous other certification programs operate today, including:

- **Smithsonian Bird Friendly Certification:** It certifies that the coffee is 100 percent organic and shade-grown, with agroforest preservation that fosters a healthy migratory bird environment.

- **Utz Certification:** It promotes sustainable farming by encouraging farmers to implement and maintain solid agricultural practices and manage responsibly with respect for people and the planet.

- **Rainforest Alliance Certification:** It helps integrate biodiversity conservation, community development, and implementation of effective planning and farm management systems to ensure a sustained livelihood for farmers and their families in coffee origin countries.

- **USDA Organic Certification:** It ensures an agricultural system utilize organic farming methods and approved substances to produce food that supports biodiversity and enhanced soil health.

Washed processing is the most common method used in Peru. The typical taste of Peruvian coffee is somewhat soft in character. Tastes are clean, sweet, and a bit heavy, distinguished by mild acidity and complexity.

Venezuela

From the beginning of coffee production in Venezuela sometime around 1730, to 1793, the number of plantations increased, but it wasn't until the early 1800s that coffee established itself as an important crop. The peak was in the 1920s, but petroleum began to overcome coffee as a significant revenue producer. An industry price drop in the 1930s dealt a severe blow to the Venezuelan coffee industry.

Finding coffees from Venezuela (see Figure 6-14) is somewhat rare; both Arabica and Robusta are cultivated there. The four main growing regions are

>> Ciudad Bolivar

>> Maracaibo

>> San Cristobal

>> Valencia

The Arabica coffee that is grown in Venezuela has taste profiles of sweet, rich, and low acidity with washed coffee processing as the standard.

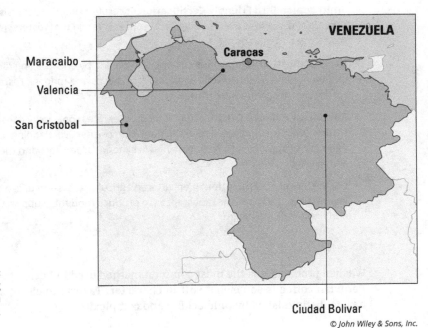

FIGURE 6-14:
Coffee-growing
regions in
Venezuela.

Ciudad Bolivar

© John Wiley & Sons, Inc.

Examining the Caribbean's Impact on Coffee

Some mountainous locations in the Caribbean are ideal for growing coffee. The three islands I look at in this section have experienced a diversity of political and environmental turmoil, and their success with coffee has been impacted by factors related to both.

Cuba

Although coffee in Cuba started around 1748, it wasn't until a group of French settlers arrived in 1791 that you can see a real crop yield. By 1827 coffee eclipsed sugar in revenue results. However, with minimal government support the coffee industry didn't flourish. Subsequently a political revolution and communist control kept coffee production rather bleak.

Today a small amount of both Arabica and Robusta coffee is grown on small family farms in three regions (as shown in Figure 6-15):

>> Escambray Mountains in the middle of the island

>> Pinar del Rio in the West

>> Sierra Maestra Mountains in the East

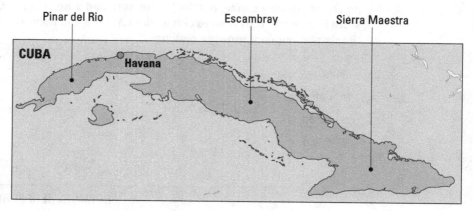

FIGURE 6-15: Coffee-growing region in Cuba.

© John Wiley & Sons, Inc.

Most of it is processed naturally and sun-dried. Taste is low in acidity and heavy bodied. Some coffee from Cuba is exported to Japan.

REMEMBER

Most significant relative to coffee is the nomenclature that exists around drinks and preparations referred to as Cuban coffee. You often see Cuban coffee offered in U.S. cafés despite a trade embargo that forbids any import of Cuban coffee to the United States. Generally, these preparations are derived from Cuban heritage but contain no coffee from Cuba:

>> **Café con leche:** Coffee with milk is a beverage combining strong coffee, often espresso, with very hot milk, usually in equal parts.

>> **Café cortado:** Also an espresso and steamed milk coffee beverage. Usually small, 4 ounces.

>> **Café Cubano:** Coffee sweetened by adding sugar to the grounds.

Refer to Chapter 12 for more detail about these and other types of coffee drinks. You can also check out www.dummies.com and search for "Coffee For Dummies Cheat Sheet" for more discussion about different drinks.

ON THE
WEB

Dominican Republic

Coffee started in the Dominican Republic in 1735 on the portion of the island that was then Spanish-controlled and called Hispaniola.

By the late 1700s coffee had risen in agricultural importance and was second only to sugar. In the 1800s an area called Valdesia (see Figure 6-16) became the most noted for growing coffee, but during the 19th and 20th centuries, farmers diversified into other crops besides coffee. Both Arabica and Robusta are grown here in the six predominant growing regions:

>> Azua

>> Bani

>> Barahona

>> Cibao

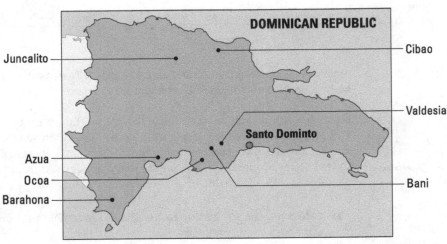

FIGURE 6-16: The Dominican Republic.

© John Wiley & Sons, Inc.

» Juncalito

» Ocoa

Today a large percentage of the small annual coffee crop is consumed domestically, but some does export to the United States, Europe, and Japan. Washed coffee processing is the standard, and the taste profile for Dominican coffees is mild with low to medium acidity and a clean finish.

Jamaica

Even though coffee production started in Jamaica in 1728, not until the 19th century did the island really begin to see significant coffee production. And not until 1950 when the Jamaican Coffee Board was formed did Jamaican coffee begin to see growth. At the same time coffee drinkers worldwide acknowledged improvements in Jamaican coffee taste and quality.

The Jamaican Coffee Board has had considerable success in marketing the Blue Mountain coffees, all Arabica, known for their sweetness and clean taste profiles. Jamaican coffees found their niche, and for a few years they had the world's most celebrated coffees.

REMEMBER

However, recent quality and distribution advancements in Central and South America as well as African coffees have made the competitive scene for coffee far more intense. As a result, the mild and sweet Jamaican coffees, although still prized, don't enjoy anywhere near the singular edge they had in the late 1900s and early 2000s.

Jamaican coffees are processed using the washed processing method (refer to Chapter 2), and the coffee is celebrated for its balanced, smooth taste characteristics and its limited to nonexistent bitterness.

Delivered in signature wooden barrels, Blue Mountain coffees are sold with names that identify their quality and the altitude in which they're grown (see Figure 6-17):

» **Jamaica Blue Mountain:** Refers to certain *parishes* (named Portland, St. Andrew, St. Mary, and St. Thomas, these are the main units of local government) and a growing elevation of 1,500 to 3,000 feet.

» **Jamaica High Mountain:** Refers to coffee grown between 1,500 to 3,000 feet.

» **Jamaica Supreme:** Also referred to as *Jamaica Low Mountain,* this refer to coffees grown at lower elevations.

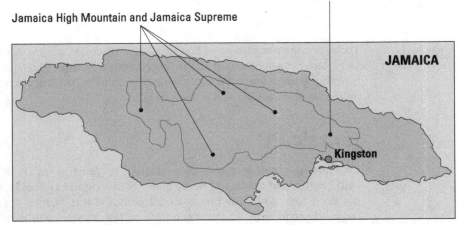

Blue Mountain Area
Portland, St. Andrew, St. Mary, and St. Thomas Parishes

Jamaica High Mountain and Jamaica Supreme

JAMAICA

Kingston

FIGURE 6-17:
Coffee-growing
regions in
Jamaica.

© John Wiley & Sons, Inc.

Getting the Aloha Feel: Hawaii's Influence on Coffee Production

Coffee had a brief and unsuccessful beginning in Hawaii in 1817, but in 1825 profitable farming of coffee got a foothold. Coffee production on all the islands remained small until the 1980s when the sugar business collapsed and coffee really took off.

Kauai and Kona (see Figure 6-18) are most known for coffee, with Kona clearly the most celebrated globally. Coffees from Hawaii are often among the most expensive because of the wage protections for the workers in this U.S. state. Hawaii is the only state where coffee is cultivated commercially.

Washed coffee processing is the dominant method used in Hawaii, and the taste profile most associated with Hawaiian coffees is mild acidity, medium but pronounced body, and limited complexity of flavor.

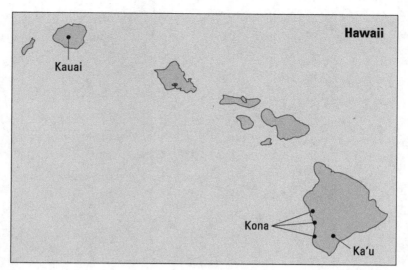

Kauai

Hawaii

Kona

Ka'u

FIGURE 6-18:
Coffee-growing
regions in Hawaii.

Chapter **7**

Discussing Africa

A coffee world tour stop in the African continent offers a unique history as well as perhaps the most exotic and noteworthy flavors seen in all the world's coffees. More than any group of origin countries, Africa offers a possible glimpse of the future. Numerous countries in Africa (refer to Figure 7-1 for an overview of the continent) highlight a mix of cultural upheaval and modern infrastructure growth, and in every place, a human investment in growing and processing coffees for export, building brighter futures for those who are invested in it.

This chapter examines the past coffee contributions of the African continent and how the areas continue to impact coffee production today.

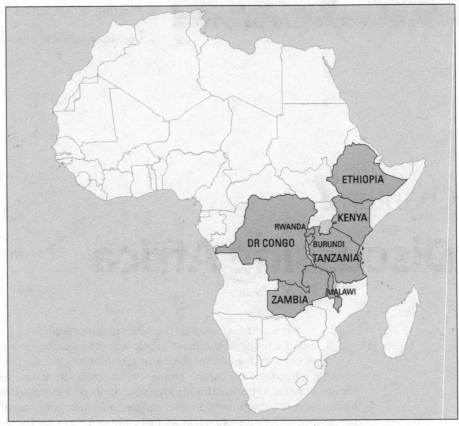

FIGURE 7-1:
Africa.

Looking Closer at Northeastern Africa

Northeastern Africa is where coffee began centuries ago, and the coffee countries here continue to be central to the industry today. Specifically Ethiopia and Kenya, representing two of the most well-known source countries in that geographic region, have a significant history in terms of coffee. This section explains in great detail how Ethiopia and Kenya have influenced coffee in the past and how they continue to influence coffee today and will do so in the future.

Ethiopia

Ethiopia, located in northeastern Africa, is one of the most reputable coffee producers in Africa. Although the country has encountered challenges politically and climate-wise, coffee continues to be an important part of the country's economy with coffee exports accounting for more than 30 percent of the country's exports. In fact, coffee Arabica, the coffee plant, originates in Ethiopia.

The following sections investigate the current state of coffee in Ethiopia and a look back at the history.

Coffee today in Ethiopia

Today the system for coffee in Ethiopia has more flexibility than it historically did, which allows for individual coffees to be sourced and exported. The following define how coffee is sourced in Ethiopia today. These terms often appear as part of the descriptions that the roaster provides to consumers:

» **Forest coffee:** Also referred as *wild coffee,* this category represents roughly 5 percent of the coffee grown in Ethiopia.

» **Plantation coffee:** This category involves the most intense cultivation because land is cleared, planted, and managed and can be represented by both larger farms and *smallholders* (small farms following a small-scale agricultural model). This group represents about 10 percent of total output.

» **Garden:** Also referred to as *semi-forest coffee,* this category describes coffee plants transplanted to and growing near farmers' homes. Output of garden coffee represents about 50 percent of coffee grown in Ethiopia.

» **Semi-forest coffee:** This type involves some management of the growing environment in ongoing pruning and supplemental plant cultivation. It represents about 35 percent of the crop output in Ethiopia.

Notable regional names in Ethiopia include (see Figure 7-2)

» Harrar (also known as Harar)

» Jima (also known as Jimma)

» Lakempti (also known as Lakemte or Nakemte)

» Limu

» Sidamo

» Yirgacheffe

REMEMBER

Taste descriptions of Ethiopian coffee range from fruity, defined by candy or tropical notes, citrus, sweet, to elegant and remarkably complex.

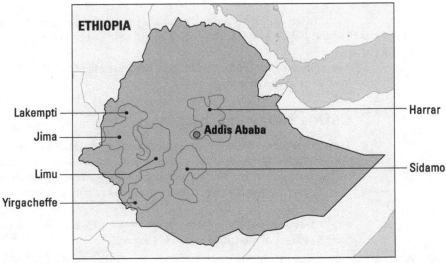

FIGURE 7-2:
Coffee-growing
regions in
Ethiopia.

Huge differences in natural growing environments, combined with washed and natural processing output that is today experiencing more experimentation and variation in individual methodology than has ever been seen in processing, contribute to a range in taste and unique sensory qualities that has never been seen before in Ethiopian coffees.

Coffee's history in Ethiopia

Ethiopia is often recognized as the birthplace of coffee (as I discuss in Chapter 3), although historians have provided well-founded caveats that coffee probably grew first in Sudan. When coffee initially was recognized as a crop with value for consumption in Ethiopia, more than likely it was so that it could be eaten, not as any kind of prepared beverage.

Consider this look back to see the journey of coffee production in Ethiopia:

>> **1600s:** Wild production and undeveloped industrial infrastructure highlighted the early years of coffee growing. Some production exports started during the 17th century.

>> **Early 1800s:** Coffee from Enerea, one small part of today's Ethiopia, saw an increase in export. Two names that established prominence in this time were Harrari and Abyssinia — two common grades — the first coming from Harrar, the second more widely seen throughout Ethiopia.

>> **1950s:** This decade represented a splendid growth period for the Ethiopian coffee industry. The government created an oversight Coffee Board, and economic and technological advancements continued.

>> **1970s:** A civil war and a coup overthrew the Ethiopian government. A famine devasted the country, the population was in turmoil, and elements of what had been normal life were significantly impacted. That included the coffee crop.

>> **1990s:** This decade heralded the beginning of democracy in Ethiopia. With it came the real entry of Ethiopian coffee into the global market. Cooperatives formed and offered some protection from price volatility for the individual farmers.

>> **2008:** The creation of the Ethiopian Coffee Exchange (ECX) established significant controls on the entire trading system. Interestingly, the ECX initiated a system that forced conglomeration of crop output, which made sourcing an individual, traceable, unique parcel of coffee impossible.

Kenya

Located in eastern Africa, Kenya borders the Indian Ocean and is Africa's largest export market. Agriculture is the second largest sector of the economy with coffee being one of the top crops. The following sections examine coffee today in Kenya and a look back at the history.

Coffee today in Kenya

The grading system of Kenyan coffee reflects both green bean size and quality to help the end consumers understand what they're buying. The system includes these series of letters:

>> **E:** Elephant bean, the largest in size and seen rarely in small lots.

>> **AA:** The most common grade. Measured using a screen, these large beans often are the most expensive, although keep in mind that bean size and quality taste characteristics don't correlate.

>> **AB:** These beans are slightly smaller. This group represents about 30 percent of the annual crop.

>> **PB:** Stands for *peaberry,* a unique single bean formed where two beans would normally be. A peaberry is smaller and getting one requires careful sorting. Refer to Chapter 2 for more discussion about peaberries.

>> **C:** These beans generally aren't part of specialty, high-quality grade coffee.

>> **TT:** This grade is a combination of smaller beans sorted out using density sorting of the larger sizes. *Density sorting* means using a machine to check bean density and to separate by density.

>> **T:** These beans are the smallest, often simply broken pieces.

>> **MH/ML:** This category denotes Mbuni heavy and Mbuni light. *Mbuni* describes the dry process or natural process output and refers to bad coffee.

Kenya's coffee growing regions (refer to Figure 7-3) include

>> Embu

>> Kiambu

>> Kirinyaga

>> Kishi

>> Kyeyo

>> Machakos

>> Marakwet

>> Meru

>> Murang'a

>> Nakuru

>> Nyeri

>> Trans-Nzoia

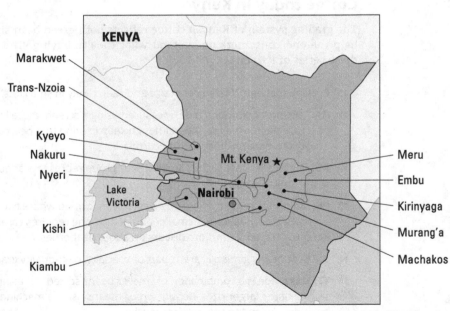

FIGURE 7-3:
Coffee-growing
regions in Kenya.

© John Wiley & Sons, Inc.

Kenyan coffees are predominantly processed using the *washed method* (fruit layers are removed from the bean after harvest, and using water, the bean is washed; refer to Chapter 2 for more about this method). The taste profile descriptions include juicy, tart, sweetly acidic, and fruit forward. The coffee tastes are often noteworthy for their fruitiness, sometimes even defined by a grapefruit or citrus quality.

Coffee's history in Kenya

Coffee production in Kenya started later than other African countries when the coffee-growing regions of the Rift Valley and Mount Kenya started in the late 1800s.

The coffee industry in Kenya made great strides in the 20th century:

>> **1930s:** Coffee in Kenya had these three developments in this decade to advance the coffee industry:

  - **1933:** The Kenya Coffee Board is established.

  - **1934:** A robust auction system for selling coffee is created.

  - **1935:** The bean size and quality grading system starts.

>> **1963:** Kenya establishes independence, which doesn't affect the coffee industry.

Today the coffee industry continues to flourish despite some minimal corruption that has impacted the free and full flow of money to coffee farmers at times.

Examining Central and Southern Africa

Coffee also has a presence in central and southern African countries. Although similarities exist across the region, there are distinct geographic and cultural differences between individual countries. In this section I take a closer look at some of the countries in this region that play a significant role in the coffee industry.

Burundi

Smallholders dominate the coffee industry in Burundi, a small country in central Africa. Generally, a mill (washing station), some of which are private and some of which are state-owned, is nearby these collections of trees.

Burundi existed under Belgian colonial rule in the 1920s when coffee was established as a production crop. With independence in 1962 the industry went private, and despite continued political unrest in the 1970s that interrupted businesses, the trend back to private has been reestablished over the past decades.

Multiple coffee growing regions exist in the country, with five being the most noteworthy. Some regions shown in Figure 7-4 include the following:

>> Bubanza

>> Gitega

>> Karuzi

>> Kayanza

>> Kirimiro

>> Kirundo

>> Muyinga

>> Ngozi

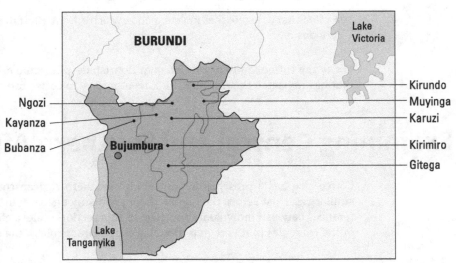

FIGURE 7-4: Coffee-growing regions in Burundi.

© John Wiley & Sons, Inc.

Over the past decade, quality has improved dramatically with the focus on the private and state-owned washing stations. Called *sogestals,* these washing stations function as both service and marketing support providers; their influence recently has resulted in some remarkably high quality, distinct coffee exports.

Unique to Africa and Burundi in particular is a traditional African variation on washed coffee processing. Incorporating a double fermentation step, the coffee is first pulped, then dry fermented for up to 12 hours before being washed and soaked for 12 to 18 hours in clean water. The coffee is then pre-dried for hand-picking before it finally is laid out on raised tables for final drying.

Congo

The provinces of Lake Kivu are home to most of the coffee production in the Democratic Republic of the Congo (DRC) (refer to Figure 7-5). Approximately 11,000 coffee farmers produce coffee in the country.

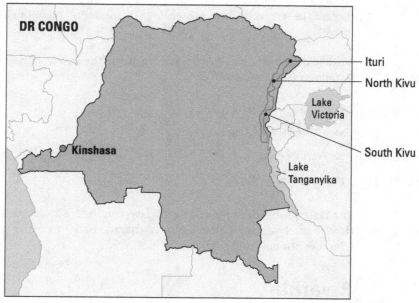

FIGURE 7-5: Coffee-growing regions in the Democratic Republic of the Congo.

© John Wiley & Sons, Inc.

Although many varieties of coffee are grown in the DRC, the two major species are

» **Robusta:** It's grown mainly in the northeast of the country such as in Isiro and in the low lands of Ubangi, Uele, Kivu, Kasai, and Bas-Congo. Robusta accounts for approximately 75 percent of the coffee grown in the DRC.

» **Arabica:** This variety is grown at higher elevations in Kivu and Ituri and accounts for about 20 percent of the total production of coffee in the DRC.

When roasters offer coffees from the DRC, the taste profile has been similar to Ethiopia or Kenya with bright acidity, herbal juiciness, and sometimes exotic fruity complexity of flavor.

Malawi

Malawi has experienced a roller-coaster existence in the years it has endeavored to establish a sustained coffee industry and export. Although coffee began in the late 1800s, it didn't take off until the late 1940s into the 1960s with a booming cooperative system. Unfortunately, much of it collapsed in 1971 after political instability.

Today a combination of smallholders and larger, commercial estates is seeing success in growing and processing increasingly high-quality well-regarded coffees.

Washed coffee processing is predominant and the noteworthy growing regions are as follows (see Figure 7-6):

>> Chitipa and Rumhi districts

>> Nkhata Bay Highlands

>> North Viphyan

>> Southeast Mzimba

The taste profile descriptions for Malawi coffees are sweet, clean, and fruity, but they're rarely as pronounced in taste characteristics as coffee produced in countries like Ethiopia and Kenya.

Rwanda

Rwanda first saw coffee planting and the start of production in 1904, but it took 13 years for things to grow. With the post-World War I mandate that established Belgian control, coffee really started and the export of coffee to primarily Belgium was firmly in place.

Everything came to a horrific end with the genocide of 1994. After the heart-wrenching situation, foreign aid flowed into the country, targeting coffee production. Many recognized coffee as a new way to move forward.

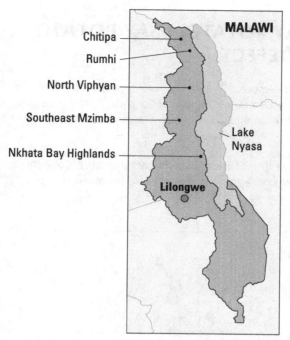

MALAWI

Chitipa
Rumhi
North Viphyan
Southeast Mzimba
Nkhata Bay Highlands

Lake
Nyasa

Lilongwe

FIGURE 7-6:
Coffee-growing
regions in Malawi.

© John Wiley & Sons, Inc.

Aid money helped build washing stations, and a laser-focused drive helped revive coffee production. Many women survivors stepped into many stages of the production with the deaths of so many men.

ON THE WEB

Check out *Hingakawa,* an original Starbucks Productions documentary at www.youtube.com/watch?v=HfSSN7aHXAg, to see firsthand how some women have responded to revive coffee production in Rwanda.

Today coffee grows throughout Rwanda, and geography defines the growing regions as follows (refer to Figure 7-7):

» The southern and western region includes an area in the mountains of Huye as well as Nyamagabe and Nyamasheke near Lake Kivu.

» The Northern region is near Kigali, the capital.

Washed coffee processing throughout Rwanda yields coffee with taste characteristics described as fruity, clean, and crisp. These coffees are increasingly gaining in recognition and popularity with consumers.

YOU SAY POTATO, I SAY POTATO
TASTE DEFECT

Sometimes a defect occurs in Rwandan coffees (also in coffees from Western Uganda, Burundi, and the Democratic Republic of Congo) that's called the *potato taste defect (PTD)*. It's rare but unmistakable because it makes the coffee taste like it has potato in it when brewed.

Scientists believe insect infestation of the cherry causes it. Coffee buyers are on the lookout for it whenever they sample coffees from these countries.

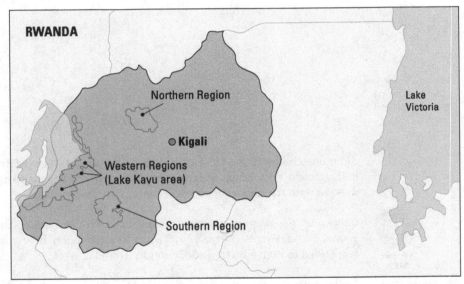

FIGURE 7-7: Coffee-growing regions in Rwanda.

© John Wiley & Sons, Inc.

Tanzania

Local storytelling heritage says coffee got its start in Tanzania in the 16th century as a boiled fruit to be smoked or chewed by the Haya tribesman. Established historical fact has coffee becoming a cash–producing crop for Tanzania in the early 1900s. German colonial rule, a transition to British control, and intermittent collaboration and conflict between the Haya and Chagga tribes all played a part in the further development of a coffee industry in Tanzania.

Continued turmoil occurred throughout Tanzania in the 1900s and 2000s, which affected the productivity and quality of the coffee production (of both Robusta and Arabica).

Most recently, the State Coffee Marketing Board has eased control to individual smallholders. Coupled with work to overcome coffee-damaging diseases, Tanzania now exports some fine coffees, although they're offered in limited amounts.

Figure 7-8 shows Tanzania's growing regions:

>> **To the north:** Situated near Mount Kilimanjaro and the border with Kenya, including the Kilimanjaro, Tarime, and Arusha areas

>> **To the south:** Mbeya and Ruvuma

>> **To the west:** Kigoma

All areas use washed coffee processing, and the taste characteristics include moderate to bright acidity, berry and fruit notes, and a clean finish.

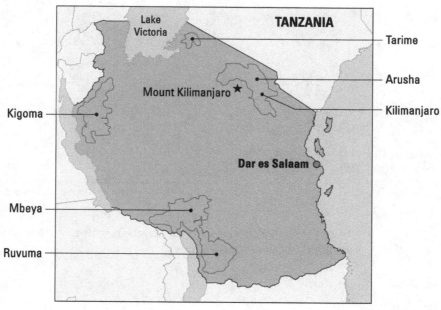

© John Wiley & Sons, Inc.

FIGURE 7-8: Coffee-growing regions in Tanzania.

Zambia

Missionaries coming from Kenya and Tanzania brought coffee to Zambia in the 1950s. In the 1970s and 1980s the industry experienced some growth, but investment and government involvement supported the controversial Catimor hybrid varietal over the Bourbon varietal, and quality and subsequent demand suffered.

Coffee production in Zambia is currently a balance between large estates and smallholders with washed processing widely used. Although regions aren't defined, coffee is primarily grown in the area near the Muchinga Mountains and an area closer to Lusaka, the capital city (as Figure 7-9 shows).

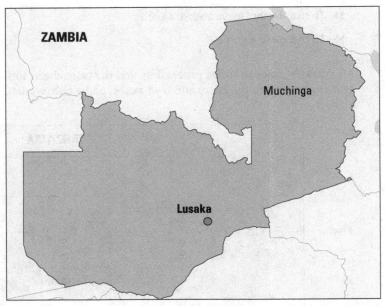

FIGURE 7-9: Coffee growing in Zambia.

© John Wiley & Sons, Inc.

Taste profile descriptions for the Zambian coffees include sweet and floral and exhibiting a clean, fruitlike finish.

Chapter **8**

Addressing the Eastern Hemisphere and Asia Pacific

Perhaps no region provides you with a broader spectrum of taste profiles than the Eastern Hemisphere and the Asia Pacific. I've often wondered how one region can be responsible for such different coffees. For example, compare a benchmark Indonesian coffee known for its rich earthiness to a noteworthy Vietnamese crop known for its sweetness and often complex flavor.

This chapter explores the Asia-Pacific (see Figure 8-1) growing region and examines the importance of climate, topography, and diverse growing practices in some exceedingly large countries and in contrast some incredibly remote, smaller ones. I hope this chapter helps simplify what choices you like or dislike.

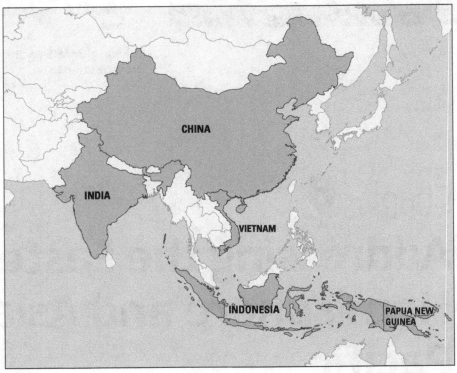

FIGURE 8-1:
Asia Pacific.

Examining the Countries Biggest in Size, But Not in Coffee Production

China and India may be the world's largest countries with the most people, but in terms of coffee production, they're not nearly the largest suppliers. However, they're both making strides in producing some top-notch coffees that are impacting the coffee industry in a good way.

The following sections consider these two countries and how they're making their presence known in the coffee world.

China

Coffee cultivation in China began in the late 19th century thanks to French missionaries who introduced it in the Yunnan province. What would be considered the modern Chinese coffee cultivation industry began in 1988 when the Chinese government, World Bank, and the United Nations Development Programme joined to collaborate on the introduction of coffee growing in the region. Nestlé and Starbucks also initiated coffee growing ventures in Yunnan to encourage the cultivation of coffee.

Today the Yunnan province is still responsible for most of the domestic coffee, which includes both Robusta and Arabica cultivated for commercial export, with the main regions being as follows:

>> Baoshan

>> Dehong

>> Pu'Erh

Refer to Figure 8-2 for a map of the growing regions in China.

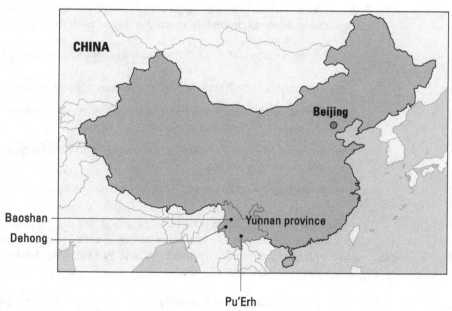

FIGURE 8-2:
Coffee-growing
regions in China.

© John Wiley & Sons, Inc.

Specialty coffee really began to gain notice in Yunnan after 2009, and although limited quantity is available, more than a decade later, the industry is watching China as a potential future source of both increasingly special coffees.

Washed processing of Arabica crops is predominant and taste notes feature sweetness, moderate complexity, medium acidity, and body.

India

Legend says Baba Budan taped seven beans to his chest and secretly transported them from the Yemeni port of Mokha to an area in India now known as Chikmagalur, beginning a long-standing tradition of coffee growing that has seen inconsistent. Despite the burgeoning growth of coffee in India, especially since the earliest planting, tea drinking still reigns in the world's second most populated country. Even as early as the 18th century tea overshadowed coffee, not only in the number of people who drink it but also in the amount grown.

In 1942 the Coffee Board of India was established, and government involvement resulted in dramatic increases in production of both Arabica and Robusta coffee.

Growing regions in India are in the south in these four states as Figure 8-3 shows:

>> **Andhra Pradesh:** A state located in the Eastern Ghats Mountains

>> **Karnataka:** The state with the largest production, where Bababudangiri, Chikmagalur, Coorg, and Manjarabad are located

>> **Kerala:** A southwestern state where you can find Travanacore, Wayanad, as well as the Malabar Coast

>> **Tamil Nadu:** A state farthest south where Pulney, Nilgiri, and Shevaroy are located

Coffee processing in India is primarily washed and dry process (sun-dried or natural). One unique process exclusive to India, called *monsooning*, dates to 1858, a time of huge exports of coffee from India to Britain. Refer to the nearby sidebar for more about monsooning.

Taste profile descriptions for Indian coffees vary widely given the multiple processing methods. The washed are thought to be mild, a bit acidic, and pleasantly clean. The naturals are a bit heavier. Neither is particularly complex.

MONSOONING EQUALS WOODEN BOXES SOAKED WITH WATER

Unavoidable circumstances resulting from harvested green coffee needing to be transported by ship from India to Europe during the time when the monsoon season occurred led to the start of Monsoon Malabar.

Early Monsoon Malabar Coffee was exported in wooden boxes, which often became soaked with water when shipped in the monsoon months. The coffee developed strong, sometimes polarizing taste changes, although some consumers really enjoyed it. Although the process is controlled today, coffee processed this way is still available and prized by some.

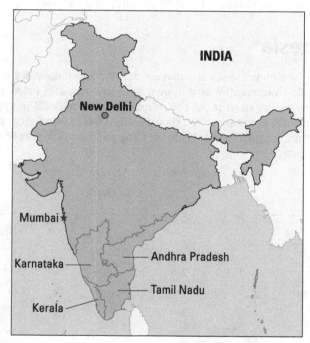

FIGURE 8-3: Coffee-growing regions in India.

© John Wiley & Sons, Inc.

The Heavy Hitters: Identifying Some Traditional Coffee-Producing Countries

A friend and coffee buyer once remarked to me that Indonesian origins are true examples of the sometimes-miraculous efforts that go into making it possible for consumers' easy access to coffee. This area of the world is both geographically astonishing, remote, and as diverse culturally as could be imagined.

That coffee has been grown, processed, and exported from places like the familiar Java, or the islands of Sumatra, Sulawesi, and Papua New Guinea is a miracle of sorts.

Additionally noteworthy is Vietnam's rise from a tiny coffee production center to the world's No. 2 producer of Arabica and Robusta varieties.

Indonesia

Indonesia (see Figure 8-4) is a diverse archipelago known for beautiful beaches and Komodo Dragons. It's also known for some rich and heavy coffee. Although coffee growing began in 1699, coffee export really took off in 1711, thanks to the Dutch East India Company. Even though only Arabica was first cultivated, Robusta was added not long after and continues to be an important part of the total exportable crop today.

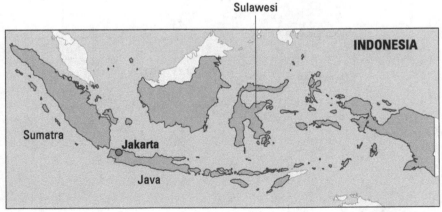

FIGURE 8-4: Coffee-growing regions in Indonesia.

© John Wiley & Sons, Inc.

CALLING COFFEE JAVA

Chapter 3 discusses the history of coffee and how Dutch entrepreneurial efforts acquired and transported coffees from remote places back to the Netherlands and then to the world. In those incredibly early days, Ethiopia and Kenya in Africa were significant supply countries as were the islands Sumatra, Sulawesi, and Java.

A significant producer at that time, Java had plenty of coffees flowing into the supply chain. Bags from there were marked with the country's name, Java. Thus, a nickname was born. Many people even today still refer to coffee as java, and not just coffee from the island of Java.

Quality and consistency issues have plagued coffee production from Java over the past 30 years or so, and you rarely see Java coffee being offered for sale.

Coffee got its first foothold on the Indonesian island of Java, and by 1750 it was also grown on Sulawesi. By 1888 North Sumatra in the Lake Toba region was established and eventually coffee was growing in Gayo, near the Lake Laut Tawar Lake region.

The following sections take a deeper look at what makes Indonesian coffees so unique and different.

Processing coffees unusually

Perhaps the most unique aspect of coffees coming from Indonesia is the processing method that is a variation and hybrid combination of the traditional washed and natural processing methods, known as *giling basah*, which translates to "wet grinding." This processing, which is most associated with Sumatra, is actually seen across Indonesia. It's referred to as semi-washed or wet hulled in the industry.

The process begins with fresh harvested, ripe cherry that the farmer depulps using small, easily transported pulping apparatus. This depulping removes the outer skin but leaves much of the *mucilage*, or sticky layer, just beneath the skin. The beans are gently handwashed and then gathered and stored, usually overnight. The following day the beans are taken to a wet hulling machine where the parchment, still quite damp, is removed. At that point, the coffee is taken to dry.

Recognizing some unique Indonesian tastes

The taste characteristic descriptions for semi-washed Indonesian coffees are quite different from those coffees in washed Latin American or African countries (see Chapters 6 and 7 for more details about these geographic areas). Heavy, full-bodied, syrupy, and rich are often terms used to describe Indonesian coffee, whereas terms like acidity or tartness are rarely seen. These coffees are often thought to be stronger although that term can be misleading if you find bright and acidic strong.

Kopi luwak is the Indonesian coffee produced from the collected droppings of civet cats that have eaten coffee cherries. In cleaning, processing, and finally drying, the result looks quite ordinary. The reputation has led to an inflated price as well as a significant amount of counterfeit product. More troubling to many is that some unscrupulous players are now caging the civet cats to control what was originally a wild process.

REMEMBER

Another distinctly flavored coffee is aged Sumatran coffee, which is most successfully started using Indonesian coffee, specifically from Sumatra. What makes it unique is the consistency of the green bean and its processing from cherry to bean. Evidence shows the importance of monitoring and limiting the time between harvest and the roasting and consumption of coffee each crop year (refer to Chapter 11 where I discuss how freshness affects flavor).

Aged coffee provides yet another chapter within the coffee story. It dates back to the Dutch traders and their success at acquiring freshly harvested green coffee beans in their travels. Dutch trading ships were often at sea for quite some time before they had filled their ships holds. As a result, sacks of green coffee sat exposed to the below-deck elements for months. When the cargo was unloaded and inspected, the traders were surprised to see that the color of those green beans had gone from fresh green to a darker, almost brownish jade green color. When the coffee was roasted and brewed, it gained a cedary, woody, almost musty quality. In my experience, of all the unusual coffees I've tried over the years, aged coffee was the most different — it has an almost cedary, somewhat woody taste. You rarely see aged coffee for sale today, although aged coffees are an ingredient in the bean blend recipe for Starbucks Christmas Blend each year.

Papua New Guinea

You may be tempted to group Papua New Guinea together with its neighbor to the east, but geographical proximity aside, Papua New Guinea (refer to Figure 8-5) has a coffee heritage and industry unto itself, and the exported product represents some of the most unique coffees available in the world today.

Although efforts to begin planting coffee in Papua New Guinea were unsuccessful in the late 1800s, by 1926, 18 estates had been established in the Highlands areas near Mount Wilhelm and Mount Hagen. The original seeds for those estates were brought from Jamaica's Blue Mountain. Today smallholder farms prevail in Papua New Guinea, and washed processing is predominant.

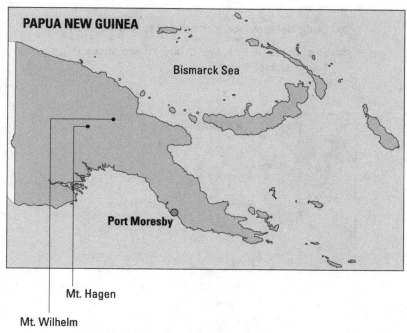

FIGURE 8-5:
Coffee-growing regions in Papua New Guinea.

Mt. Hagen

Mt. Wilhelm

© John Wiley & Sons, Inc.

The taste descriptions for Papua New Guinea coffees include sweetness, bright acidity, savory, with an unusual rich mouthfeel, and significant complexity.

Vietnam

From coffee's introduction into Vietnam by the French in 1857 until 1910, coffee was grown but enjoyed minimal success as a commercial endeavor. At the end of the Vietnam War in 1975, a coffee industry existed on a small scale. However, things quickly changed. Over the next 15 years increasingly large tracts of land were allocated to coffee cultivation. As a result, Vietnam established itself as an influential player, becoming the second largest producer of coffee in the world.

Both Robusta and Arabica are grown in Vietnam, and coffee production areas dot the country (see Figure 8-6):

>> **Central Highlands:** Home to numerous provinces growing Robusta

>> **Dalat:** In the Lam Dong region, known as an excellent source of quality Arabica

» **Dong Nai province:** Northeast of Ho Chi Minh City

» **Son La, Thanh Hoa, and Quang Tri provinces:** Home to numerous small-holder Arabica farms

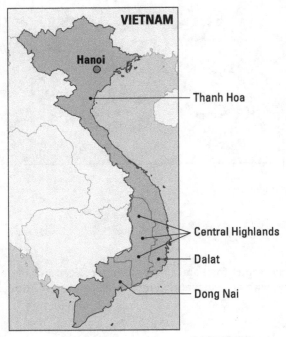

FIGURE 8-6:
Coffee-growing regions in Vietnam.

© John Wiley & Sons, Inc.

Arabica coffees from Vietnam are quite diverse in flavors, and although washed processing is dominant, the differing acidity, complexity of flavors, and increasing quality are noteworthy.

REMEMBER

Although only 3 to 5 percent of all coffee grown in Vietnam is Arabica, the production quantity is high enough to make it the 13th largest Arabica producing country in the world.

Yemen

The presence of coffee in Yemen can be traced back to the 15th and 16th centuries when people started drinking coffee near Yemen's Port of Mokha. (Refer to Chapter 3 for more discussion on the rich history of coffee.) Today that coffee production is the world's oldest.

REMEMBER

You'll see variations of mocha, like moka and mohka, in descriptions of coffees from other origins. Note that the powerful tasting, exotic coffees of Yemen gave rise to the use of mocha to describe similar coffees sourced elsewhere. Just because it uses the term doesn't mean it's from Yemen.

REMEMBER

Very early in the history of coffee trade exporters blended coffees from multiple origins. The result of blending coffee from Mokha with coffee from the Indonesian island of Java was Arabian mocha java blend — two distinctly notable origins and two recognizable coffee flavor profiles combined to become the world's first blend.

Land for growing is at a premium in Yemen, and coffee is mostly grown on terraced land at high altitude. In addition, water is quite scarce. Combine the high altitude with the water scarcity, and you get an incredible number of plant varietals that produce a complexity of unrivaled flavor profiles.

The primary growing regions are in the western part of Yemen (refer to Figure 8-7). Most famous is Sana'a, known for growing the Mattari heirloom varietal of Arabica. Other notable regions include

>> Hajjah

>> Mahweet Sa'dah

>> Raymah

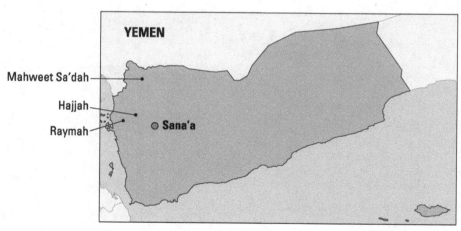

FIGURE 8-7:
Coffee-growing regions in Yemen.

© John Wiley & Sons, Inc.

Because of water scarcity, natural, sun-dried processing has always been predominant.

The flavor descriptions of coffee from Yemen, perhaps the most unusual and exotic coffees you can experience, include complex, wildly fruity, and piquant. They can be some of the most polarizing of coffees, with some coffee drinkers finding them absolutely the best, whereas others find them undrinkable.

4

Roasting Coffee

Chapter **9**

The History of Roasting

I n order for you to enjoy a coffee someday that you describe as the greatest, most memorable you have ever had, you need to understand how roasting has contributed to what you drank and enjoyed. A look at the history of roasting can help you understand and appreciate the rather mysterious transition that occurred starting with edible coffee and then to roasting and how roasting has evolved to where it is today.

This chapter explores the history behind the beginning of roasting. This chapter also digs into the history of dark, medium, and light roasts and what you may find valuable when looking at the taste profiles you like and how roasting plays a key part in them.

Understanding How Roasting Started

As I discuss in Chapter 3, Kaldi, the legendary goatherder and his herd of wayward goats tasted coffee beans, birthing the tasty and energizing edible. People in Kaffa, an early modern state in what is now Ethiopia, created the custom of chewing coffee beans. That practice moved to Harrar and Arabia by enslaved Sudanese who chewed coffee to help survive the arduous journeys of the Muslim slave trade routes.

Although the details of how roasting started remain elusive, coffee historians believe in 1258 A.D. Sheik Omar began roasting at Ousab in Arabia. He had been forced out of Mokha into the desert and was expected to succumb from starvation. He ate coffee fruit to survive and found it quite bitter. Roasting then improved the flavor and adding water made it even more desirable.

The first historical recognition of coffee being roasted to then brew in the more modern style was in the 15th century Sufi shrines in Yemen where coffee was ground and brewed. Green coffee beans were cooked or roasted brown (see Chapter 2 for more details). The browned seeds were then ground, infused in hot water, and coffee as it's known today was created.

Examining What Roasters First Used

Although roasters today use intricate tools and techniques to roast coffee (refer to Chapter 10 for more information), the beginning roasters weren't that complicated.

In the early days of roasting, the process was quite simple as utensils from the Ottoman Empire and greater Persia document. Roasters used a frying pan with a long handle, which allowed the roaster to hold the beans in the pan over the fire (refer to Figure 9-1 for an example).

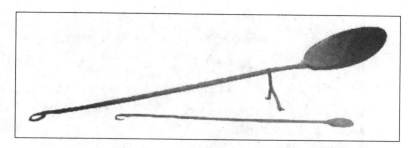

FIGURE 9-1:
A coffee
roaster from
the 15th century.

Source: www.wordpress.com

Ethiopians used this same method in their coffee ceremony. In fact, Ethiopians have the longest historical and cultural attachment to coffee, and their ceremonial preparation and consumption of coffee together in celebration of life is complex and noteworthy.

The ceremony is conducted even today, and when possible, it involves open, hand roasting of coffee in a frying pan, grinding it, and finally steeping it with hot water. Chapter 16 discusses a traditional Ethiopian coffee ceremony if you're interested in attending one.

Developing Roasting into a Business

What the Ethiopians initiated as a daily ritual with coffee and a cultural connection exploded onto the world as coffee became increasingly more popular and widespread globally. Industrial and technological advancements and a burgeoning entrepreneurial spirit led to the introduction of many new commercial ventures, and coffee roasting was among those. Small shops and even European street vendors roasting coffee gave way to bigger operations, and an industry was born, which the following sections discuss.

Starting slowly

The 1800s saw the true beginning of coffee as a major commercial industry with the invention of larger and larger machines used to roast coffee, like the wood stovetop coffee roaster in Figure 9-2. Businesses in England, Germany, and the United States scaled up coffee roasting to meet increasing consumer demand as the numbers of patent submissions for roasting machines increased.

Source: www.rootsimple.com

In the 1900s U.S. consumers enjoyed the growth of some of the most famous brand names in coffee as Martinson's, Chase and Sanborn, Hill's Brothers, Maxwell House, and Savarin all established brand presence as coffee roasters with the burgeoning consumer base.

European roaster development was less significant and on a smaller scale with fewer marketable brands because roasters were less centralized. However, Norway's Friele was surely recognized, as was Douwe Egberts in Holland, with roots as a coffee business going back to 1753.

You can also trace a trend to this time that would become hugely significant in later roasting styles. Those European countries that drank the most coffee per capita — Sweden, Norway, Denmark, and Finland — demanded higher quality and a lighter finished roast.

During this time, the French, Italians, Portuguese, and Spanish coffee drinkers liked darker roasts. Some of that preference was attributable to the sometimes use of Robusta with Arabica as a blend where the darker roast would mask some of the harsher tastes found in Robusta.

Moving to roasting specialty coffee

The birth of specialty coffee occurred in the late 1960s when Alfred Peet recognized an opportunity to offer high quality, carefully roasted whole bean coffees to consumers of mass-produced, commodity grade Arabicas. (Chapter 3 discusses Peet and other roasters who influenced specialty coffee.)

Specialty coffee basically refers to the highest quality coffee that is available today. Flip to Chapter 13 and read about Erna Knutson, the person responsible for giving this type of coffee its name. Prior to Peet, coffee roasting was focused on efficiency and cost more than the taste quality of what was created.

All roasters make a conscious choice about what their coffee will give the consumer in the cup. They do that through the process of taking the coffee from green (raw) to some level of cooked — light, medium, or dark. See Chapter 10 for more on roasting and how they taste differently.

Peet's style of roasting is directly attributed to the Italian love of dark roast. Similarly, that same style can be traced to Starbucks. In 1971 when the three founders of Starbucks started, they learned to roast from Peet, and the Italian dark roast heritage was continued.

The debate between light versus dark roasts became a predominant and enduring theme as more and more specialty coffee roasters have entered and compete for consumers. Every roaster can trace its roasting style to these early days in the coffee business.

MY EXPERIENCE WITH COFFEE AND ROASTING

I grew up asking for coffee even as a youngster, and my mother, who in the mid-1950s, brewed both with a Corning Brand percolator and Chemex for special occasions, was always indulgent enough to share a bit, albeit heavily laced with cream and sugar. My early decision-making, consistent with many consumers of the 1960s, just ahead of the birth of specialty coffee, was simply one in which cream and sugar or black was the primary question. My introduction to specialty coffee came through the Coffee Connection and the lighter roasted coffees so celebrated by its founder George Howell.

That introduction also opened the complexity of deciding, as multiple coffee origins and blend creations were added. Although I understand now that variation in roast was highlighting the skills of those early artisan roasters, to me, a new consumer, my roast preference remained consistent with what I was drinking — lighter. Not until the mid-1990s did I begin to explore mail ordered coffees from both Peets and Starbucks. I experienced what many coffee drinkers do when they taste something other than their usual — I had a chance to taste many coffees from roasters who went darker. I experienced rather immediate dislike, as though something was wrong with the coffee that tasted different. I understand now that I was beginning to learn how crucial the roasting style of the brands and individual roaster are to the coffee I was exploring.

You can see some roast variation in the late 1960s and early 1970s, as The Wet Whisker, which would become Stewart Brothers and then eventually Seattle's Best Coffee, could trace its smooth roasting style to the Northern European method and lighter color finish. George Howell's Coffee Connection in Boston, established in 1971, was also a proponent of lighter roasting.

Today, you and I join all coffee consumers in having access to the widest range of unique coffees that are roasted in an almost endless variety of styles and colors. The signature that a roaster puts on a coffee yields an equally endless number of taste possibilities.

Chapter **10**

Roasting for Flavor

R oasting coffee beans may seem simple. After all, you're just placing some green, unroasted coffee beans into a hot environment and then watching as they turn from green to brown, and then become darker and darker until, at just the right color, you take them out and cool them off. However, roasting isn't that easy. You may get lucky and come up with a good result, but more than likely, you won't. That's why most people don't roast their own beans and why professional roasters who know what they're doing after years of experience roast coffee to perfection. This chapter explores what the roaster — the chef who is cooking the coffee — must know.

More specifically, this chapter explains how roasting is both an art and a science and how the steps taken in the process, a time-temperature continuum, impact the flavors that you eventually experience when your roasted coffee is ground and brewed. This may seem like a lot to understand in your quest for that amazing, memorable-tasting experience. The truth is, more than likely you depend on roasters because you aren't going to roast coffee yourself. However, knowing what goes on in the roasters' quest for the ideal acidity, body, flavor, sweetness, and balance can help you understand and choose the right coffee.

Walking the Fine Line of Roasting: A Balance between Artistry and Science

In order to arrive at a coffee experience, many people have to complete many tasks along the way. One of the crucial tasks is for a roaster (the person) to essentially cook the coffee (roasting), usually in some sort of special oven (the roaster).

The following sections detail the early efforts of the roasters to create coffee for consumers and an important transition that signaled a change in roasting style, making taste the new top priority or goal for some roasters.

Saving money, time, and raw materials

Roasting is crucial to changing the hard, green coffee beans into something that can be ground and brewed. Until the introduction of what's referred to as specialty coffee in the late 1960s, roasters focused all their technological advancements on completing this process with the greatest efficiency and limited loss — the actual weight loss the bean undergoes when heat drives away moisture.

THINKING ABOUT DECAF?

A small but mighty group of coffee consumers want their coffee without caffeine. They generally represent about 5 percent of coffee drinkers and they deserve options. Coffee beans get their caffeine removed before they are roasted. These three methods provide good options of green, unroasted, decaffeinated beans for roasters to roast.

Decaffeination happens using three methods:

- **Chemical** involves the use of methylene chloride. The chemical and coffee are placed in contact, and when the chemical is extracted it holds onto the caffeine.

- **Swiss Water** applies water to organic green coffee. When the water is separated from the beans, the caffeine goes with the water.

- **Natural** applies carbon dioxide gas to the beans. When the gas is removed, so goes the caffeine.

The process, while an incredibly complex technological achievement, can be simplified by imagining the green coffee immersed and soaked in an element (the chemical, water, or carbon dioxide). When that element is removed it carries the caffeine with it.

A roasting machine, referred to as a roaster (see Figure 10-1), depends on a heat source to make the process happen. Wood was used in the earliest roasting machines, but gas is now used in modern machines. Of course, roasters had incentive to keep this key resource use to a minimum to save money.

FIGURE 10-1: A roasting machine.

After minimizing fuel use and the costs to make heat, another important consideration was weight loss during roasting. Anything that is cooked begins to lose weight through either water loss or other elements being cooked away. Coffee can have considerable weight loss through losing moisture. Commercial roasters strive to keep this loss at a minimum.

TECHNICAL STUFF

You and I can see evidence of this weight loss on a retail shelf. Because my years in coffee were spent primarily with Starbucks and more than likely you're familiar with its stores, I use Starbucks for this example. Look at a shelf of displayed one-pound bags of roasted coffee. The bags, all one pound in weight, don't all look like they're the same size or have the same amount of beans in them. Darkest roast Starbucks French roast stands quite a bit taller on the shelf than a bag of one of the lighter roasts. The reason: The number of beans needed to fill the darker roast is greater because they have become lighter by being roasted darker. It takes more of them to get one-pound's worth.

Moving past the color

With the development of specialty coffee, roasters put aside the rather simple incentives of efficiency and loss prevention. Their prime incentive was to use the developing science of cooking this green bean, and to couple it with an almost artistic, aesthetic approach to draw out the coffee-specific characteristics.

Based on their decisions and actions during the time-temperature continuum, the beans would turn from green to brown, dark brown, or almost black. However, landing on a color wasn't enough for roasters.

Early specialty roasters discovered that the range of possibilities was virtually infinite. That surely was a burden equal to the delight they must have experienced as they experimented. Replicating a roast of an individual coffee proved to be more difficult than they had anticipated.

They learned quickly that any variations within the time and temperature, from batch to batch, with the same green coffee would result in dramatic taste variability. They could achieve consistency only by adopting a rather systematic, scientific approach. Science joined the roasting process.

Roasting, Step by Step

The process of roasting can be as simple as placing green coffee beans in a frying pan, or as complex as utilizing one of the technologically sophisticated roasting machines of today. In this section, I dig into a step-by-step overview of the process of roasting so you have a better understanding of what roasters do to your coffee. Roasters often describe this process as the *roast profile*.

Step 1: Loading or charging and drying

In this first step, the roaster stages a measured batch of green coffee beans, usually in an external attachment called a *hopper,* that serves as the doorway into the heated interior. At a specific moment, the roaster introduces the batch to the inside where the heat is.

REMEMBER

The first variable in roasting coffee is the starting or *charge* temperature. Some roasters prefer a temperature as low as 320°F (160°C), whereas others start hotter at 425°F (218°C). The generally accepted temperature is somewhere around 350°F (177°C).

The temperature drops slightly as the cooler coffee beans are introduced, and the heat source is set to control both how low the drop is and how quickly the reheat occurs inside the heated interior. This step includes the drying process, which begins as the beans absorb the heat and become hotter (known as the *endothermic state*). At about 347°F (175°C), the beans transition to an *exothermic state* — they're so hot that they're really heating themselves. The roaster — the person roasting — adjusts to maintain temperature control.

Step 2: Yellowing

In this step, the coffee loses its green color and turns yellow. The heat is driving out the moisture of the bean, and the bean is beginning to expand. A thin, papery skin, called the *chaff*, flakes off the bean near the end of this step.

Step 3: Popping or cracking — the first time

The beans quickly change to a light brown in this step, and water vapor and carbon dioxide build up inside the beans. This browning step signals the beginning of something called the *Maillard reaction*, which refers to when the sugars and amino acids in the beans react to create aromas and color compounds known as *melanoidins*.

REMEMBER

When the pressure gets intense enough, the beans undergo an explosion where they almost double in size, and that moment also features a discernible noise — a kind of popping or cracking noise, hence the step name. If the coffee is finished at this moment and you ground and brew it, you might find it to be sweet, nuanced, and complex or perhaps grassy, tart, and undeveloped.

Step 4: Developing or monitoring

The coffee continues to change in this step. The beans darken and internally become more active as the heating process expands them and moisture is released. The roaster — the person — is in close contact with the coffee during this step and watches the coffee by extracting small samples to gauge color, smoke, and some oil drops that appear. These oil drops result from oxidation and *lipids* — the oils in the coffee bean — within the beans coming to the surface as the beans heat up.

REMEMBER

Another significant change, accompanied by a slightly less pronounced but discernible noise, occurs during this step. The beans break down in the heat, and the browning increases, usually when the beans reach 414° to 424°F (212 to 218°C). If the roasting finishes at this step, the beans will be balanced, sweet, complex, and even deeper into specific fruit or food flavors, especially those flavors that the roaster hopes are inside the bean, and that the process of roasting has now revealed.

Step 5: Finishing

Any time after the first crack but certainly before the coffee beans burn and turn to ash the last step of finishing occurs. This last step involves the roaster stopping the process and releasing the coffee into a cooling tray attached to the outside of the machine below the heating drum to cool. The finish is often tension-filled as the coffee and roaster have almost danced up to the moment, as she has manipulated the temperature and monitored the time and bean color to arrive at exactly the intended sweet spot.

Deciphering What the Different Roasts Mean and How They Taste

Today you're faced with an incredible opportunity to choose between coffees, and the roast level is an important factor in whether you like or dislike a coffee. Your taste preferences are key, and the more you understand about the different roasts, the more informed decisions you can make. Because there are no industry standards for naming coffees, trying to figure out the meaning of many of the names appearing on roasts can be confusing (see Figures 10-2 and 10-3). I'm here to help you make a coffee selection that speaks to you.

Roasting the green bean has turned it to shades of yellow and eventually some shade of brown. The resulting color is achieved by exposing the green beans to a combination of temperature and time in that hot temperature.

TIP

When determining which roast you want to taste first or early on in your exploration, I suggest avoiding the *edges* (the very lightest or very darkest). Start with medium roasts from a few vendors and explore within this middle range. The coffees in that range will undoubtedly be varied, but my experience has been that even with that more limited roast range, you can begin to identify notable differences. After you experience those *a-ha* moments, you can begin to identify the characteristics that might warrant extending the exploration to the lighter or darker edges.

FIGURE 10-2:
A roaster putting
beans into the
hopper.

Source: Juan Jose Napuri Guevara/123 RF

REMEMBER

There are no rules about roasting rules. Different coffees roasters roast within each range, and roasters can argue endlessly about what specific roast level is exactly right for a certain coffee. There are also no rules about what a roaster calls light, medium, or dark. For example, in the context of Starbucks coffees, Intelligentsia's darkest roast would be considered light. Each roaster has developed its own style and has searched for individual coffees that it feels can be roasted with that style to create notable experiences for its customers.

The following sections discuss what the different roast levels mean when referring to tastes in high-quality specialty coffee.

Light roasts — bright and flavorful

Lighter roasts often accentuate acidity or tartness, sweetness, fruitiness, limited body, syrupiness, or *mouthfeel*, that is they're more watery or lighter feeling. These coffees hit you with their taste, but the finish is limited. They aren't oily and include light-brown roasts, which are preferred for milder coffee varieties. Some notable light roasts in order of roast level are

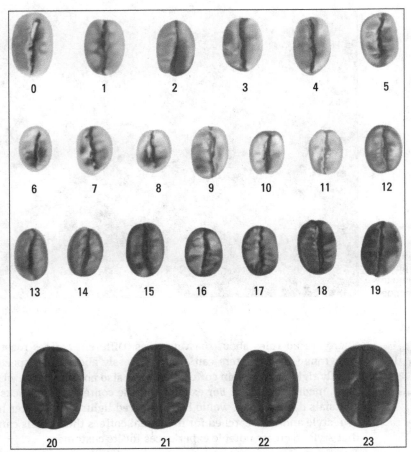

© John Wiley & Sons, Inc.

FIGURE 10-3:
The color range, from green to French roast.

>> Light City

>> Half City

>> Cinnamon

Medium roasts — balanced and complex

These roasts are medium brown with a stronger flavor than light blends, although they're still non-oily. They begin to gain a bit more mouthfeel; that is they're a bit thicker or syrupier and less watery. They can present some acidity or tartness, but to a lesser degree than light roasts. Coffees roasted at this level are the most popular, as they avoid the edges, sitting nicely balanced in the mid-roast range with some acidity, body, and flavor. Some notable medium-roast blends in order of roast level include

>> City

>> American

>> Breakfast

Medium-dark roasts are a richer, dark-brown color with some oiliness. They often have a bittersweet aftertaste. Full City is one notable medium-dark roast blend.

Dark roasts — uniquely flavored

Dark roast blends have black beans with an oily surface and a pronounced bitterness. Any tanginess or acidity has been reduced or eliminated at this roast level. They dramatically highlight an almost burnt, smoky flavor not found in the light and medium coffees. Depending on the bean and its level of darkness, there might be a hint of acidity, and complexity as with a medium roast, but it's often subtle.

In the darkest-roasted coffee, acidity and tartness are gone, nuanced flavors are diminished, and the smoky, charred taste is dominant. I've heard these coffees described as being either like a sweet campfire marshmallow or simply burnt, depending on whether that person liked or disliked the taste.

Some notable dark roast blends in order of roast level are

>> High

>> Continental

>> New Orleans

>> European

>> Espresso

>> Viennese

>> Italian

>> French

5

Preparing Coffee and Espresso

Familiarize yourself with the different ways that coffee is brewed and how the brewing method you choose can affect the end taste.

Find out more about extraction — in other words, getting coffee to drink out of adding water to coffee grounds.

Get the lowdown on the simple steps that guide you to great coffee and espresso results.

Define the uniqueness of espresso as a brewing category by exploring the machine, bean, grinders, and the barista's role.

Dive into milk and milk steaming and find out what the foam is all about.

Put the espresso and milk together and understand what the drink names mean.

Chapter **11**

Exploring the Brewing Methods and Mastering the Tricks

M aking a delicious cup of coffee often seems like an impossible task for someone who is just starting out. How often do you walk into your favorite coffee shop, order a brewed coffee, take a sip, and think to yourself, "How do they do this so well? Why can't I make a cup of coffee this good at home?"

This chapter answers that first question with an explanation of the way brewing works and how the barista extracts the goodness from the bean to create a cup of coffee for you. As for that second question, the answer is, "You can!" This chapter outlines the most common brewing methods and explains how they function, so you can decide what will work best for your situation and taste.

Understanding Extraction

A lot of thought goes into that delicious cup of coffee, and the barista or server who made your coffee has been trained to do so. The person behind that perfect brew uses quality coffee equipment, exceptional coffee beans, and well-honed expertise. But you can have those things, too.

REMEMBER

The first thing to understand is what is happening when coffee is brewed: how coffee is dissolved into water. The scientific terminology is *extraction*. Extraction begins with water being brought into contact with ground coffee. What you take out of the ground coffee is what makes the clear brewing water turn brown. If you get this extraction process right, the result should be tasty.

Sounds simple enough, but this effort is informed by choices that you must make during the process. Like a chef in the kitchen, you must choose from among a number of variables that together will influence the final creation, the finished coffee.

Focusing on the Basics of Coffee Brewing

Certain standards and measurements influence your final cup of coffee, and they've been established over time to help determine whether a brew is considered good. But there's a lot of subjectivity as well. As with any chef's creation, no single perfect result exists. You probably remember an ideal cup of coffee that you've enjoyed, and chances are that you compare every cup you buy or brew to that ideal cup.

REMEMBER

Does that mean all rules are meant to be broken? Not exactly. If you ignore the established standards and measurements, you run the risk of creating some really bad-tasting coffee. The point is that there's a huge range within what is considered an acceptable result. As a brewer, you can discover what you can manipulate and when, in order to create the right variations and achieve predictable, and almost certain, results.

TIP

Think of following the brewing process that I dissect here as being like a laboratory scientist beginning an experiment. Nail down a specific decision related to every variable, based on what I recommend for each one. Finish a brew, taste it, and decide if it's what you had hoped for or expected. If you feel something is lacking or you didn't get what you wanted, experiment until you do. In this section I explain what goes in a cup of coffee and offer some ideas about what you might change to create a different result.

Identifying the variables that make a cup of coffee

A cup of coffee consists of these important variables. I explore how you can adjust them as you see fit:

>> **Coffee-to-water ratio:** This is your recipe. Consistency and good results will depend on careful measurement of coffee and water. I dig deeper into this idea in the section, "Following a recipe," later in this chapter.

>> **Grind:** From an almost powder-like consistency to very large particles, this variable begins with knowing what grind is recommended as appropriate for your brew method and discovering how variations can impact your results. I discuss the different brewing methods later in this chapter in the "Examining the Brewing Methods" section.

>> **Contact time:** Brew method recommendations have you targeting a time frame of three to five minutes. The type of brewing method you choose and your preference are also significant.

>> **Temperature:** The simple recommendation is to brew just off the boil, but the water you use and its exact temperature also play a part.

>> **Turbulence:** Stirring and pouring style have a direct impact on results. Think of a flight when the seat belt sign and pilot warn you about an upcoming bumpy ride. That's turbulence in coffee as well. Something impacts the stillness and eventual taste, and you control that in hand brewing.

>> **Water quality:** Water is around 98 percent of your finished coffee brew, and whether you choose tap water or a different water source, you'll need some of the simple info I provide in the next section to understand the impact water has on the end result.

>> **Filter type:** The filter is what is in between your coffee and the water. Your choice is determined by your brewing method you choose. Sometimes filters are made of metal, mesh, or paper; your choice is an important variable.

The following sections delve deeper into these variables to help you brew your ideal cup of coffee.

Starting with the water

Brewing success begins with some fundamentals and essential elements that you must consider as you brew. Water is the most abundant component of the finished product — comprising roughly 98 percent — so that's a logical place to begin.

TIP

A general rule is that if you're drinking the water from your tap at home, it's probably fine to use that water when you brew your coffee. If your tap water doesn't taste good on its own, it will most certainly create brewed coffee that's not good. The following sections examine the importance of water, including the mineral content and water temperature you should use.

Mineral content

You turn on your tap and out comes water. In most situations that water is as perfect as the municipality it's coming from can ensure, and the municipality is constantly analyzing it. It naturally contains some minerals, including calcium, magnesium, and potassium.

Your city or town processes your tap water by purifying it and adding some minerals to achieve a balance for you. Water experts say that the ideal mineral balance is around 150 parts per million (ppm) when brewing coffee, but there is tremendous variation, and that impacts your results when you make coffee.

If you have well water and want use it to brew coffee the same general rule is true. If you like the taste when you drink the water, you'll probably be satisfied with coffee brewed using it.

REMEMBER

Why are minerals so important to brewing coffee? *Distilled water* is water that has had all the minerals taken out. Think about the process of distilling as a matter of leaving behind empty space in the water. Adding minerals in this way takes up more space in the water. The opposite of distilled is mineral water, which is often sourced naturally and sold to consumers who want more minerals. As I discuss in the earlier section, "Understanding Extraction," the extraction process takes something out of the coffee grounds and puts it into the water.

Here's what happens to your coffee when the mineral count is either too low or too high in the water you use.

>> **Overextracted:** When water has a low mineral content and a low measurement in terms of ppm, there's simply too much empty space to fill with the substances you're extracting from the coffee, resulting in a bitter taste.

REMEMBER

You might be thinking that if clean, pure water has an ideal mineral content, distilled water would be perfect. Distilled water has had almost *all* its mineral content removed, and those minerals serve an important function beyond affecting the taste of the water. Distilled water measures at approximately 9 ppm, which means virtually no minerals.

>> **Underextracted:** Brewing with water that has an extremely high ppm or mineral content — what many people call *hard* water — also doesn't have enough room left for the extracted coffee, resulting in a sour taste. Hard water measures at approximately 250 ppm.

Temperature

In order to extract what you need from the coffee grounds into the water, use hot water. The best water is just boiled, or 195° to 205° Fahrenheit (90° to 96° Celsius) at the point of contact with the coffee). You may have heard about cold-water coffee brewing; I discuss that method in the section "A few more options," later in this chapter.

Adding the coffee

The other ingredient in a brewed cup of coffee is, surprise, the ground coffee. However, several of the following variables related to your coffee can impact the extraction process.

Freshness

Begin with the freshness of the coffee. After all, coffee is the roasted seed of a fresh fruit. As with any fresh food, there's a period when it's at its peak, and only a limited time when it remains at its peak. Air (oxygen), light, heat, and moisture are the enemies of freshness, so whatever you can do to protect the coffee from exposure to those factors will help maintain its integrity.

The following factors can affect your coffee's freshness.

>> **Where you store your coffee:** Some people think storing coffee in the freezer or refrigerator seems like a reasonable idea, because that's what you do with a lot of other fresh foods. Not with coffee, however. Moisture is present in the fridge, and moisture in the bean combined with freezing will harm the consistency of the coffee. Moving the coffee from cold to room temperature and then putting it back can also make it taste bad.

TIP

Your best practice for storage is a cool, dry environment, which often means the bag in which you originally received the coffee. Wrap it or roll it tightly to force out extra air to help prevent oxidation and then tuck it in a cool, dry cabinet.

>> **How long you store your coffee:** You may be surprised; coffee is at its peak of freshness for about seven to ten days after it's opened or first exposed to air, not prying eyes.

REMEMBER

Many roasters use incredibly sophisticated packaging, including such features as flavor-locking valves, nitrogen flushing prior to sealing, and multiple-layer roll stock. By packaging the coffee this way, the roasters can guarantee a significantly extended shelf life — but *only* until you open the bag. Then the clock starts ticking faster, and you're in that freshness period of seven to ten days.

>> **Whether your coffee is whole bean or ground:** Most professionals agree that grinding your coffee just before you use it is the best way to get fresh coffee. Consider that exposure to air is an enemy of freshness, and grinding coffee beans increases the coffee's exposure. That's why coffee that's stored after grinding just seems to fade faster.

Grind size

Grind size is a highly important brewing factor to consider. That's because the size of the ground coffee particle impacts how hard or easy it is to extract just the right amount of flavor compounds from that coffee into the water.

This following list describes popular grind sizes and their uses:

>> **Extra coarse:** Used for cold brew coffee or cowboy coffee. Similar in size to coarsely ground peppercorns.

>> **Coarse:** Used for French press, percolators, and by some cuppers for sampling. Similar in size to sea salt.

>> **Medium coarse:** Used for Chemex and Clever brewers. Similar in size to rough beach sand.

>> **Medium:** Used for flat bottomed drip coffee makers, cone-shaped pour-over makers, AeroPress, and siphon brewers. Similar in size to regular sand.

>> **Medium fine:** Used for cone-shaped pour-over brewers. Finer than sand but not as fine as espresso grind.

>> **Fine:** Used for espresso. A bit finer in size than table salt.

>> **Turkish:** Used for Turkish coffee brewed in the ibrik. A powder-like consistency similar to flour.

The exchange between the water and ground coffee takes place in the brewing device, so every brew method has a recommended grind size. That ideal grind is intended to optimize the contact between the ground coffee and water for a certain time. Coffee that is too finely ground for a particular brew method will over-extract, whereas if it's too coarse, the opposite occurs.

Following a recipe

The recipe to make the perfect cup of coffee is simple: water plus ground coffee. However, following the recipe is a tad more complex. You need to know how much water and how much coffee to use, how long to keep them in contact, and how to get them apart, separating the grounds from your finished coffee when you're done.

COMING UP WITH THE PERFECT RECIPE: ERNEST EARL LOCKHART

All modern brewing knowledge derives from the work of Professor Ernest Earl Lockhart, who was a faculty member of the Massachusetts Institute of Technology's food technology department in the early 1950s.

The good professor was the first director of the Coffee Brewing Institute, worked to help define coffee quality, and eventually established the Coffee Brewing Center, which was based in the United States until the 1970s. The National Coffee Association (NCA) commissioned him, and he created what the *SCA News* describes as "a quantifiable method to track the consistency of each brew."

More insights come from the Specialty Coffee Association (SCA). The SCA has chapters all over the world. It's a nonprofit organization with thousands of members representing all parts of the specialty coffee industry. Producers, roasters, baristas, and others join together in the SCA to celebrate "openness, inclusivity, and the power of shared knowledge." You can find out more about the SCA at https://sca.coffee.

As early as the 1940s, Professor Ernest Earl Lockhart (read more about him in the nearby sidebar), and more recently the Specialty Coffee Association (SCA; refer to Chapter 14 for more information about this organization), developed a simple recipe: 2 tablespoons of coffee for every 6 ounces of water. If you prefer metric measures, that's 10 grams of coffee to 180 milliliters of water, or 55 grams per liter. You often see that expressed as a ratio of 1 to 18, or 1:18.

Examining the Brewing Methods

Your brewing method is an important part of making a great cup of coffee, because different methods introduce additional control factors to consider. Various devices have their own control factors governing such things as turbulence, flow rate, and contact time.

Another important aspect is the filter, which keeps the grounds separate from what you eventually drink. Refer to the section, "Identifying the variables that make a cup of coffee," earlier in this chapter for more about these different variables that make a great cup of coffee.

In the following sections, I discuss some different devices and the techniques that each device requires.

Exploring immersion methods

With any brewing method, coffee and water come together for a defined period of time, and then they're separated. What's left is the liquid you consume and the grounds you clean up later. Following are three immersion methods you can try.

Cupping

Perhaps the simplest immersion brewing method is *cupping*. Coffee companies around the world use this method, as tasters evaluate coffees for potential purchase and do the work of quality control by testing through tasting at different stages of production (Figure 11-1 shows an example). The SCA provides a specific protocol for cupping, but the general idea is that a small, measured amount of coffee, ground precisely, is combined with a measured amount of hot water in a bowl or cup for a specific time.

FIGURE 11-1:
Cuppers taste
test coffees.

Source: Gumpanat Thavankitdumrong/123 RF

The combined ingredients are smelled and stirred gently, once. The grind size is large enough so that the coffee grounds will saturate and sink, leaving the coffee toward the top of the cup or bowl. The person doing the cupping can then dip out a spoonful of coffee and taste it.

French press

If you want to sip a whole cup of coffee, then French press immersion is great (see Figure 11-2 for an example).

FIGURE 11-2:
A French press.

French press also goes by these other names:

>> Cafetière

>> Cafetière a piston

>> Cafeteria

>> Coffee plunger

>> Coffee press

>> Press pot

TECHNICAL STUFF

Italian designer Paolini Ugo came up with one press idea, and designers Attilio Calimani and Giulio Moneta patented it in 1929. A similar design was patented earlier by two Frenchmen, Mayer and Delforge, in 1852. The first presses were made in France, which is why so many people call them French presses.

REMEMBER

This method uses carefully measured doses of ground coffee and water at the correct temperature. The coffee dose is ground medium to coarse. Extraction begins when the ground coffee and water are combined in the cylindrical vessel, which is often made of glass, but sometimes plastic or metal.

Thorough extraction will result only if you completely mix the ground coffee and water, and successful brewers develop a knack for pouring the water in a way that ensures this saturation occurs. They may even stir the coffee and water at the start. The recommended brewing time is four minutes, and then you push the plunger.

The plunger is fitted with a screen that looks like a fine mesh window screen, although it is also sometimes plastic. Plunging that screen through the liquid forces the grounds to the bottom but leaves the liquid above the screen and pourable. Some people who brew with a French press add a last step of decanting the liquid into a second vessel in order to maintain flavor integrity.

REMEMBER

Coffee that is brewed with a French press is often noteworthy for its fuller flavor, body, and richness. This is because the coffee is coarsely ground and the screen mesh, the filter, is porous enough to allow quite a lot of the solids to pass through into the liquid. That creates a signature feature of the brewed coffee: residual grounds left behind in the empty cups of those who have finished their coffee.

Clever brewer

A variation on immersion is known as the clever brewer. This brewer is similar to the French press in that the measured water and coffee sit together for a determined amount of time.

The difference is, as soon as the time is up, you place the brewer on your cup. The apparatus is designed so that the bottom opens and allows the coffee to pour out into the cup, carafe, or vessel below. This filtering method uses a paper or cloth filter instead of mesh, which makes for a cleaner cup of coffee.

Using the force of gravity: The pour-over

A different variation, referred to as the *pour-over*, uses gravity to control the process as the brewer pours the water onto, and eventually through, the coffee grounds. Here are some details.

Comprehending the basics of a pour-over

A pour-over (as shown in Figure 11-3) makes a single cup or small batch of coffee, and most people experience this brewing style when they have coffee at a restaurant, coffee shop, or convenience store. Think of the familiar urn or airpot-style dispensing container, and recognize that the machine the establishment used to brew the coffee was an automatic pour-over that makes one or two gallons per brew cycle.

REMEMBER

Pour-over coffee is easy-peasy. If you're ready to make the perfect cup or pot of pour-over coffee, make sure you have the following equipment and ingredients:

- » Paper, metal, or cloth filter
- » Apparatus (cone-shaped, wedges, flat-bottomed) to hold the filter
- » Carafe, cup, or vessel on which to place the cone
- » Ground coffee
- » Water
- » Kettle to heat, hold, and pour water
- » Scale (optional)

FIGURE 11-3: A pour-over.

Source: Elena Veselova/123 RF

Making your own pour-over

Here is my favorite recipe for brewing. Some steps may vary, depending on the specific recipe and your preferences. Variables include the amount of ground coffee and water, whether you stir and for how long, and how long you wait between pours. When you're ready to make your own, just follow these steps.

1. **Measure the coffee.**

   This is where your recipe begins to unfold. The amount of ground coffee you begin with determines the total quantity of water to be poured. I use 40 grams, a recipe ratio of 1:18, and thus my target for a final weight is 720 grams. I can adjust this final volume weight up or down to brew a bit less or more if I have company. I keep the 1:18 and calculate accordingly.

2. **Heat the water.**

Water will comprise more than 98 percent of your finished brew, so you need good, clean water. A general rule is that if you're comfortable drinking your tap water — that is, it has no off tastes, like chlorine, rotten egg, salty, or metal — then you can brew with it. If it has any quality that makes you question it, more than likely it will impact your brew in a negative way. The water should be boiling when you begin pouring.

3. **Fold the paper filter and place it in the cone (holder).**

You may notice that most paper filters have a seamed edge, and the fold should be on that edge. Folding the filter allows it to sit more easily in your cone.

4. **Pour the heated water over the paper to rinse the paper and heat the vessels.**

This step is super-important because you don't want your coffee to get a taste of paper, which it almost always will if you skip the rinse step. Another benefit: The rinse will serve to heat up your cone and the vessel the coffee will eventually drip into.

5. **Discard the rinse water.**

6. **Put the measured ground coffee into the paper cone.**

Tap the cone to level the coffee grounds in your filter so that in your first pours, you get good saturation and good coverage.

TIP

7. **Pour 50 to 100 grams of water over the grounds to saturate.**

This step is vital to get all your grounds wet. Just don't pour too much water. The grounds will begin to expand a bit; this is called the *bloom.*

8. **Wait 60 seconds.**

During this time, called the *blooming,* you may see some bubbling in your coffee and water as carbon dioxide leaves the coffee.

9. **Pour more water.**

REMEMBER

The total brew time will be three to five minutes. Pour 150 grams more water, bringing the coffee and grounds up in the filter paper. At this point you're at about 250 grams total. You can either gently stir five to six times, or perhaps gently roll the entire brew cone to create a swirl. At about the three-minute mark, pour another 250 grams of water, and around the 3:45 mark, finish by pouring the remaining water to hit the target total of 720 grams. Enjoy.

THE INVENTORS OF THE POUR-OVER: NOTEBOOK PAPER, CHEMISTRY, AND GLASS

Here are a few people who are known to have invented some form of the pour-over.

- **Using a piece of her son's notebook paper:** Melitta Bentz, a resident of the German city of Dresden, brewed fresh coffee at home each morning. Her son tells a story in a 1949 edition of the German publication *Der Aufstieg* that his mom was often dismayed by the grounds or sediment left in her cup when she finished her percolator-brewed coffee.

  One day she solved the problem by using a piece of her son's school notebook paper, placed into an old tin pot in which she had punched holes. She added ground coffee, poured her hot water over it, and the liquid dripped through into her cup. Cleanup was easier than with her old coffee ground–covered brewer — the paper went in the trash along with the grounds. Her invention led to a variety of pour-over brewing concepts. The following figure shows her first round pour-over brewer and the paper filters she used in 1910.

© The Melitta Group

- **Relying on his chemistry background:** Peter Schlumbohm was known to be eccentric and visionary, always looking at ways to improve or enhance daily activities, and making coffee was one of them.

  With his background in chemistry, he understood the concept of extraction. He recognized that using a thicker paper might enhance the results, and he created a

(continued)

sketch of an hourglass-shaped vessel that would hold the paper into which he placed the coffee and through which he poured water (see the following figure of his Chemex design, which is still used today). His finished coffee flowed into the bottom. His invention became one of the 300 patents he submitted and is recognized today for both its beauty and the high-quality coffee results.

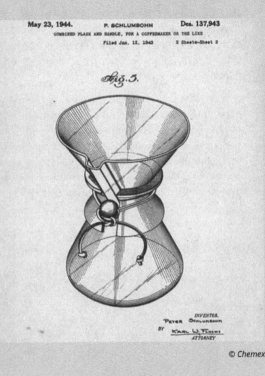

May 23, 1944.   P. SCHLUMBOHM   Des. 137,943

COMBINED FLASK AND HANDLE, FOR A COFFEEMAKER OR THE LIKE

Filed Jan. 12, 1943   2 Sheets-Sheet 2

Fig. 5.

INVENTOR.
PETER SCHLUMBOHM
BY
KARL W. FLOCKS
ATTORNEY

© Chemex

- **Manufacturing glass:** Another noteworthy pour-over invention comes from Japan, where Hario, a long-respected manufacturer of laboratory glass, had made its way to coffee by creating a glass filter coffee siphon in 1949.

  Hario achieved its most noteworthy recognition in the field of coffee in 2005 with the creation of the Vector 60 (see the following figure). Named for the 60° angle of its cone, Vector 60 got the attention of the coffee world for its unique internal design and for the designer's attention to materials that would enhance extraction. First made of ceramic, glass, and plastic, the ultimate model was copper, which lent itself to high thermal conductivity and enhanced extraction.

© Hario USA

Keep in mind that quite a few designs are available for the cone that holds the paper, as well as different papers to use for filters. You can even purchase some metal insert cones that eliminate the need for paper.

A few more options

Here are three more ways you can choose to brew and enjoy your coffee:

>> **The AeroPress:** Invented in 2005 by Alan Adler, this is an increasingly popular device for brewing. Coffee steeps for a brief amount of time (about 10 to 50 seconds) and then is forced through a filter (paper or metal) by pressing the plunger through the tube.

>> **Vacuum or siphon method (see Figure 11-4):** One of the oldest brewing methods and often thought to be the most intriguing, this method uses two chambers, vapor pressure, and gravity to extract. It was invented by Loeff of Berlin in the 1830s. The design, materials, and heat source vary, but the basics are the same. Heating the water creates pressure, and the water finds its way to the upper chamber where the coffee grounds are placed. You stir, wait, and remove the heat source. A vacuum is created that pulls the brewed coffee through the filter and back into the lower chamber.

>> **Iced coffee:** Traditional iced coffee is created by adding ice to hot-brewed coffee, adjusting the recipe to be strong enough so that when ice is added, you get a tasty beverage. One general rule is to use either twice the coffee grounds or half the water to essentially create a double-strength concentrate, to which you can add ice.

>> **Cold brew:** With cold-brewed coffee, you eliminate hot water and use only cold water and ground coffee together to extract. With no heat, the extraction time needs to be much longer, approximately 10 to 12 hours. The ratio of ground coffee to water is also much higher. Cold brew is often brewed as a concentrate and diluted prior to consumption.

FIGURE 11-4:
A vacuum
brewing method.

Source: Анатолий Рабизо/123 RF

Chapter 12

Making Espresso Easier

Espresso can refer to a beverage, a coffee roast level, or a brewing method. However, it's never *ex*-presso. Although espresso is widely consumed today, many people misunderstand it. Never fear, though. I'm here to help.

In this chapter I delve into the world of espresso to discuss how it emerged, how it evolved, where it is today, and how you or your barista can use an espresso machine to create the tasty beverages featured in menus around the world.

Appreciating Italy's Contribution to Making Espresso What It Is Today

Although espresso started in Italy, today coffee drinkers all over the world enjoy this small burst of flavor. People drink it in their homes and at coffee shops for a way to warm up on a cold day or a quick pick-me-up.

A few notable Italian innovators invented the forerunners to today's espresso machines:

>> **Angelo Moriondo** of Turin is credited with having the first patent on a steam-driven, instantaneous coffee-making machine.

>> **Luigi Bezzera** of Milan was inspired by Moriondo's rapid, bulk-brewing machine, and improved on it, patenting a machine with a single-portion brewer in 1902.

>> **Desiderio Pavoni** purchased Bezzera's patent from him in 1903 and began producing machines. These machines made regular-strength single cups of coffee much more quickly.

>> **Achille Gaggia** invented the lever-driven, high-pressure espresso machine (see Figure 12-1 for an example of an early level-driven espresso machine) nearly 30 years later. This machine allowed baristas to use very small amounts of finely ground coffee to extract much smaller, intensely delicious cups of coffee.

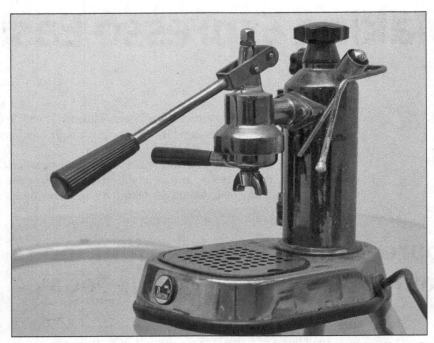

FIGURE 12-1:
The early manual lever espresso machine.

Permission from La Pavoni Europicolla

REMEMBER

The steam pressure of the early machines was roughly 1.5 to 2 BAR of pressure, and the Gaggia lever machine increased that pressure to 8 to 10 BAR. (A *BAR* is metric unit measure of pressure. Refer to the section, "Pulling a Few Shots — What's Involved When Making an Espresso," later in this chapter, where I discuss why BARs are so important when making espresso.)

Because a brewer could introduce only a limited amount of water/steam into the small chamber prior to adding pressure, the output was smaller, and so the idea of an espresso beverage being small, only an ounce or two, was born.

REMEMBER

If you've ever wondered where the saying, "pulling a shot" came from, it was Gaggia's lever machine. The barista action of pulling down the lever to load the spring release creates the intense pressure that forces the steam through the finely ground coffee and delivers a shot of espresso.

» **Ernesto Valente** worked for the espresso machine maker Faema and introduced a machine known as the E61 30 years after Gaggia invented the lever-driven, high-pressure espresso machine. The E61 boasted some impressive technological improvements:

   • **Electric pump:** The use of an electric pump to create the consistent high pressure that, in the lever machine, had depended on the skill of the barista.

   • **Heat exchanger:** A device called a *heat exchanger* that allowed for a smaller boiler, as water direct from the main water line could be drawn into a tube that ran through the boiler. This ensured that the small amount of water needed for each shot was consistently the correct, high temperature.

With these improvements, modern espresso was born.

Espresso machines today fall into four categories:

» **Traditional:** Also referred to as a *manual-lever machine,* this puts a barista in full control of *variables* including water temperature, amount of BAR (pressure) and when it occurs, grinding, dosing, tamping, and extraction timing. Refer to the section, "Pulling a Few Shots — What's Involved When Making an Espresso," later in this chapter, for more detail on the work the barista does pulling a shot.

» **Semi-automatic:** This machine uses pump-driven pressure, although the barista controls multiple variables. The machine employs automation to drive water through the group head. Grinding, dosing, tamping, and extraction time are left to the barista's controls.

» **Automatic:** This machine uses predetermined shot timing, with the barista controlling other variables.

» **Super automatic:** This machine does it all.

This range of features leads to my next focus: the different variables offered by these machines for creating espresso and espresso beverages.

Making the Perfect Espresso — the Four M's

Another gift the Italians contributed to the espresso of today was the four key elements that are needed to ensure perfect espresso. Called the four M's, they are as follows.

>> **Macchina:** The espresso machine.

>> **Macinazione:** The proper grinding of the beans — a uniform grind between fine and powdery — that is ideally created moments before brewing the drink.

>> **Miscela:** The coffee blend and the roast.

>> **Mano:** The skilled hand of the barista, because even with the finest beans and the most advanced equipment, the shot depends on the touch and style of the barista.

If all these elements come together in harmony, the result is an amazingly intense coffee experience, highlighted by a sweetness and richness that can't be equaled in any other coffee experience. I discuss these four M's in action in the section, "Making espresso, step by step," later in this chapter.

Pulling a Few Shots — What's Involved When Making an Espresso

I often marvel at baristas who display their craft behind the counter at the espresso machine and grinders. Making coffee drinks seems so simple, but like much of the coffee business, after you read about the details I share in the following sections, you can see that making a good cup of coffee is a complex process where a lot can go wrong.

REMEMBER

Here's the Specialty Coffee Association (SCA) definition of espresso: Espresso is a 25 to 35ml (.85- to 1.2-ounce — times two for a double shot) beverage prepared from 7 to 9 grams (14 to 18 grams for a double shot) of coffee through which clean water at 195° to 205° Fahrenheit (90.5° to 96.1° Celsius) has been forced at 9 to 10 BARS, or atmospheres of pressure, and where the grind of the coffee is such that the brew time is 20 to 30 seconds. You'll sometimes encounter variations at a coffeehouse, but most espresso derives from this basic recipe.

The following sections explain what you can expect at a coffeehouse, starting with a description of some of the equipment baristas use behind the counter and how they make espresso.

Identifying the equipment and all the bells and whistles

Take a quick look behind the counter at your local coffee shop or café, and more than likely you'll see a complex, semi-automatic espresso machine. Figure 12-2 illustrates the key parts of an espresso machine from a barista's viewpoint.

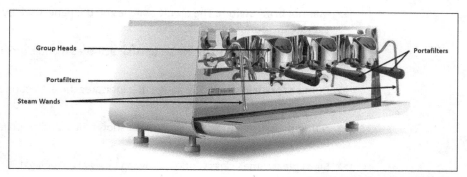

FIGURE 12-2: An espresso machine from a barista's viewpoint.

Here is a full list of points of interest on our tour of what the business side would look like:

>> **Group heads:** Where the barista places the portafilter and the source of heated water and where the pressurized extraction occurs.

>> **Portafilter:** The removable handle and basket assembly that holds the measured coffee or dose. The portafilter fits snugly within the group head, which is where the pressurized hot water eventually contacts the coffee dose.

>> **Filter basket:** Basket insert in the end of the portafilter into which the dose is measured.

>> **Basket:** Small, perforated basket inserted in the portafilter end.

>> **Retaining spring:** Metal spring that is inserted in the portafilter to squeeze the basket and keep it from falling out of the end of the portafilter.

>> **Dispersion screen:** The small screen fitted into the portafilter side of the group head to help disperse the water evenly over the dose of ground coffee at extraction.

- >> **Screw:** Holds the dispersion screen in place.

- >> **Group gasket:** The thick rubber ring that is fitted in the group head and assures a tight seal between the portafilter edge and the group head.

- >> **On/off switch:** The main switch to power the machine on and off.

- >> **Boiler:** Internal part where the water is heated.

- >> **Hot water nozzle:** Small nozzle where hot water can be accessed.

- >> **Manual fill valve:** The switch to manually add water to the boiler.

- >> **Steam valve/wand:** The stick-like appendage the barista uses to access steam in order to heat and foam milk.

- >> **Manual brew switch:** The on/off switches on the panel used by the barista to activate the pump and initiate extraction.

- >> **Automatic brew switch:** The switch that activates the full, programmed operation mode.

- >> **Pump pressure gauge:** The gauge that indicates the extraction pressure in BAR pressure measurement.

- >> **Boiler pressure gauge:** The gauge that shows the standing boiler pressure level.

- >> **Sight glass:** Small glass window showing internal water level.

If you have an espresso machine at home, make sure you have a grinder, or two, or three sitting right next to your espresso machine, because an espresso machine doesn't have an internal grinder.

Add an ample supply of coffee, a steaming pitcher to hold the milk you'll steam on the wand, a cup in which you'll place your finished beverage, and you'd have the basic elements or tools for your work.

Making espresso, step by step

The four M's that I introduce in the section, "Making the Perfect Espresso — the Four M's," are the foundation for making espresso. Whether you're the barista at home, or you're in the hands of a professional barista, envision these steps to see the four M's in action:

1. **Remove the portafilter from the group head and flush the group head.**

Removing the portafilter and running hot water through the group head starts it all off.

2. **Wipe the basket clean and dry it.**

A bit of water and perhaps some older grounds need to be cleaned off in this step.

3. **Dose and distribute the desired grams of coffee.**

The size of the measured grind particles is the first important variable. Getting your perfectly ground, measured dose of coffee into the portafilter basket is generally a function of the grinder mechanism, but you can easily scoop it in as well.

REMEMBER

Next to particle size, the most important variable is the amount of coffee used. Early baristas simply eyeballed or approximated how many grams would go into the portafilter basket, but today you can see specific basket sizes for single and double shots, and within those are baskets specific to gram weight so that the dose can be exact. Gram scale measurement of the dose every time, or at least regularly, is the rule today. A café or coffee shop will have a recipe — grams in the basket to grams in the liquid output. Remember my earlier definition: 25 to 35ml (.85 to 1.2 ounces) of liquid for 7 to 9 grams of coffee grounds.

4. **Tamp consistently, ergonomically, and level.**

While the barista uses the tamper tool to press down prior to that, she must level the dose and do a bit of cleaning around it. The actual tamping step is crucial to compacting the coffee (as shown in Figure 12-3), because the tamped coffee dose needs to be consistent and level so that the water will flow evenly through the coffee.

WARNING

This step is physically challenging for a beginner, because it takes a bit of muscle. When done incorrectly, it can leave your wrist exposed to injury (that's why doing it ergonomically is important). Watch a barista execute this step, and you'll see a variety of interesting body positions, all of them established as individual habits by baristas to hold a position for their arm that creates a kind of piston from the shoulder and elbow, not from the wrist.

5. **Clean the loose grounds from the portafilter surfaces.**

6. **Insert the portafilter into the group head and start the pump immediately, as one continuous motion (as shown in Figure 12-4).**

TIP

This moment of inserting and starting is often the most difficult for new, less-experienced baristas, because they often engage the portafilter on the machine and then do an inventory of sorts before they begin extraction. Precious seconds elapse, and the quality of the resulting shots is negatively impacted by that delay because the group head is hot. You don't want it to begin to heat the coffee, so the press the start button immediately to begin extraction.

FIGURE 12-3:
The tamping step
compacts the
coffee.

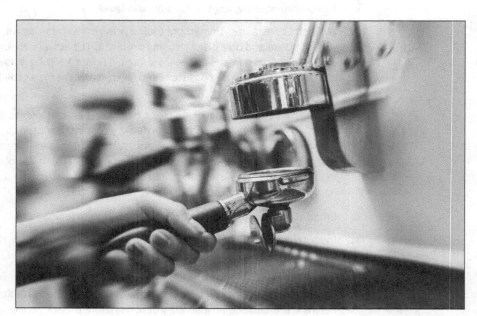

FIGURE 12-4:
A barista inserts
the tamper tool.

7. Observe the flow and stop the pump appropriately.

8. Serve the espresso, or use it to make an espresso-based drink.

9. Remove the portafilter and knock out the spent grounds.

10. Wipe the basket clean and flush the group head (rinsing is optional).

11. Return the portafilter to the group head to keep it preheated.

REMEMBER

Steps 1 to 5 outline the procedure to get the coffee situated in the portafilter, and a barista can assess its potential almost immediately in Steps 6 and 7. If the shot liquid comes out fast, the grind is probably too coarse; if it is slow or does not begin at all, the grind is most likely too fine.

REMEMBER

The breakdown of a perfect shot is well documented, and it should feature the following:

>> **Heart:** The deep, dark liquid core

>> **Body:** A golden brown liquid just above the heart that looks almost alive as it is pouring or streaming

>> **Crema:** A lighter-golden creamy layer on top

You can see the breakdown in Figure 12-5. You're ready to enjoy this shot.

FIGURE 12-5:
An espresso shot.

© John Wiley & Sons, Inc.

Adding milk or an alternative

Many espresso recipes call for steamed milk or an alternative milk (like soymilk or almond milk), also steamed. If your drink order requires milk, the barista has it nearby and ready to go. The barista steams the milk or milk alternative (see Figure 12-6) with a steaming pitcher to accomplish two tasks:

>> To add air to the milk

>> To heat the milk

Source: Aliia Arslanova/123 RF

FIGURE 12-6: The barista steams the milk with the steaming wand.

As the milk foams, it's heating up, adding volume, becoming creamier, and getting sweeter. Your barista knows the milk is perfectly steamed when it seems to have the smooth, somewhat viscous texture of latex paint (good thing it doesn't taste like latex paint!). Milk that has that look will have a rich, creamy sweetness. When it's coupled with the sharper, complex flavor of the espresso in a drink, the result is a heavenly mixture enjoyed by millions of coffee drinkers around the world every day.

Getting the right temperature for the milk is key. Between 120°F and 140°F (49°C to 60°C) is considered the ideal range. Although opinions vary widely about what this perfect temperature is, milk that's too hot (154°F or 68°C) can be affected and results in an unpleasant taste.

As to the temperature between at least lukewarm and a temperature that is too high, I've always believed that consumers knows what their individual preferences are. If you receive a beverage in a café that isn't exactly what you want, it's completely okay to ask for it be remade. (Remember a little sweetness when asking goes a long way.) In fact, I always appreciated having customers indicate if they had a temperature preference along with any other customizations. It helped me make a perfect drink for them!

Espresso and milk beverages are rarely served today without an added element of latte art. Keep in mind that the latte art pour is just a beautiful finishing touch. A great deal needs to happen before that final flair to ensure a high-quality, great-tasting beverage. Refer to the sidebar later in this chapter about latte art.

If you make espresso at home and your drink recipe calls for dairy or an alternative, make sure you have the milk ready before you pull the necessary shots. You'll want to use finished shots as soon as you make them.

Knowing What You're Ordering

Standing on the customer side of the counter at your local coffeehouse and deciding what you want can seem overwhelming. Ordering coffee used to be so much less complex in the early days. Do you want regular or decaf? Cream, sugar, or black? That was about it.

However, the world of espresso beverages introduced an entirely new language to the menu. I can recall so many conversations from the 1990s in which I helped transition coffee drinkers to the latte and cappuccino world.

The foundation to nearly all the following drinks is the same:

>> A shot or shots of espresso

>> Well-steamed milk (or some other alternative like almond, soy, or oat milk; refer to the section, "Adding milk or an alternative," earlier in this chapter for more about the milk)

Espresso solo or doppio

Espresso solo or *doppio* is the result when a shot or shots are pulled. Nothing else is added. The crema (the lighter-golden creamy layer on top) should always be obvious. The crema is created when hot water affects the ground coffee bean oils and floats atop the shot; its smooth creamy bubbles give a good indication of the quality that lies below in the body and heart layers. Figure 12-7 shows a shot of espresso.

FIGURE 12-7:
An espresso solo.

© *John Wiley & Sons, Inc.*

Ristretto

Translated from the Italian, a *ristretto* is a restricted espresso shot, which means it's smaller and stronger, because it uses less brewing water and a slightly finer grind to ensure the extraction time is adequate.

Lungo

A *lungo* is a long-pulled espresso. It involves using a bit more water, so it ends up a bit weaker. Sometimes afficionados look down on this drink, but with the right grind — often a lighter-roasted espresso coffee, ground slightly coarser — this can be a delicious beverage.

Macchiato

The name *macchiato*, which means *marked* in Italian, comes from espresso's Italian heritage. Just add a bit of milk and what you get is espresso with a dollop of milk on top. The more recent trend with this beverage is to add more milk than its earliest versions. Figure 12-8 show an example of a macchiato.

FIGURE 12-8:
A macchiato.

© *John Wiley & Sons, Inc.*

TIP

You may be confused because some roasters broadly market their beverages as macchiatos, but the drinks bear little resemblance to a real macchiato. If you're not sure what you're ordering, ask the barista to explain the ingredients.

Cappuccino

Originally derived from a Viennese, not Italian, beverage and dating to the 19th century, the *kapuziner* was a brewed coffee-and-steamed-milk combination that was poured in parts (espresso shot and steamed milk) that ended up the color of Capuchin monks' robes. The Italians and their advancements with espresso machines, great craft, and cafés gave the drink you know today a robust start.

The cappuccino (refer to Figure 12-9) is served in a small cup and consists of the following (the relative amounts of which are subject to great discussions and disagreement):

>> Espresso shots

>> Steamed milk

>> A small amount of foam

FIGURE 12-9:
A cappuccino.

© John Wiley & Sons, Inc.

The Specialty Coffee Association's accepted standard is a bit more specific:

>> A single shot (5 to 6 ounces, 150 to 180ml) of espresso

>> A topping of steamed milk foam, about ⅓-inch (1cm) thick

REMEMBER

Similar to the modern variation of the macchiato, today you can find an incredible variation in the cappuccino, with some coffee shops offering beverages as large as 20 ounces and calling them cappuccinos. In the most formal sense, they aren't, because the long-standing tradition of a rather small beverage is a well-established one.

Caffé latte

The latte (see Figure 12-10) — a top choice among espresso coffee drinkers globally — isn't Italian in origin. Rather, it's the result of coffee drinkers wanting to add some steamed milk to the seemingly strong and bitter coffee to mellow the flavor.

In fact, order a latte in Italy without the word *caffé*, and you'll just get milk. I think of this beverage more as a lightly coffee-flavored milk drink, and I often enjoy a variation in which I add or request an extra shot or two of espresso to boost the coffee flavor.

FIGURE 12-10:
A caffé latte.

Replace the steamed milk with steamed half and half for a caffé breve (see Figure 12-11).

FIGURE 12-11:
A caffé breve.

Mocha

Adding some chocolate syrup to your espresso and steamed milk makes your drink a mocha (see Figure 12-12). You can ask your barista for a dollop of whipped cream if you're decadent.

FIGURE 12-12:
A mocha.

Flat white

The flat white originated in New Zealand, or possibly Australia. No matter where it came from, the flat white (refer to Figure 12-13) has achieved global recognition as a result of the proliferation of cafés and burgeoning consumer awareness. A flat white is really a latte — often a smaller one that rarely features any foam, just well-steamed milk and perhaps a dollop of foam.

FIGURE 12-13:
A flat white.

Americano

American soldiers serving in Italy in World War II wanted to create a beverage more closely resembling the brewed coffee experience that they were accustomed to at home as opposed to the espresso they were finding in Italy. The result was the americano, which is simply an espresso with hot water added (refer to Figure 12-14).

FIGURE 12-14: An Americano.

Cortado

Originating in Spain, the cortado highlights both slightly weaker espresso shots (often found in Spain because Spaniards' preferred recipe features a longer brew) and steamed milk. A cortado is served in a small glass and consists of about 30ml of espresso with an equal portion of steamed milk.

APPRECIATING BARISTA ART

In many cafés today, you'll receive a drink that has been poured with a delightful design incorporated during the finish. This latte art, sometimes a heart, swan, or rosetta, is beautiful. I'm often hesitant to break the surface of a drink if the barista has given me a piece of art. Refer to Chapter 13 for a bit of the backstory about latte art.

Even though many baristas today make creating beautiful latte art in their final pour (free pour) or use tools to do so after the drink is assembled, I must share here with personal experience and a bit of pain that it's a skill that takes focused practice. Training for the more widely seen free-pour style begins with getting beautiful milk (refer to the section, "Adding milk or an alternative," earlier in this chapter) and timing the creation of a shot or shots of espresso. With those ingredients and a steady hand come designs ranging from a defined dot, a monk's head, and eventually hearts, rosettas, and a world of intricate and amazing creations. Here are a couple examples.

(continued)

(continued)

Photo by Major Cohen

Photo by Ryan Soeder

6

Perusing Today's Coffee Business

Identify some of the people who have made coffee what it is today and appreciate their contributions.

Explore what it takes to create a complete coffee experience at home.

Find out where you can go for beans online when you're not able to shop in brick-and-mortar stores.

Discover some great ways to stay connected to what's happening in the coffee business with books, magazines, podcasts, coffee classes, certifications, and more.

Chapter **13**

Meeting Some Coffee Trailblazers

An awesome number of people have made, and are making, the coffee business the success story it is today. In fact, estimates have stated that more than 25 million people work in the coffee business. A recent Specialty Coffee Association industry research project (`https://sca.coffee/coffee-systems-map`) identified roles in a vast coffee system map that included farmers, processors, exporters, importers, roasters, and brewers.

This chapter introduces you to a few coffee trendsetters and innovators whose names you may never have seen or heard of. I include them for the sometimes small, sometimes massive roles or contributions they've made to the current industry. They've also impacted me as an involved and curious consumer.

The list is far from complete, but I hope it advances your understanding of just what a marvelous, people-driven, passion-filled business coffee is. Many more trailblazers promise to come behind them, because the coffee industry is alive with great young visionaries.

Identifying Early Trendsetters Whose Names Have Withstood the Test of Time

I begin with some familiar names with backgrounds and stories that may surprise you, and I hope enlighten you.

James Folger

Prominent on the shelves of food shops everywhere in the world, the Folger name means coffee to many consumers, and an inspired, adventurous guy was behind it. James Folger was one of the first innovators who took coffee from a small venture to what would become one of the world's most recognizable names.

Folger was 14 when he and his two brothers left Nantucket Island in 1850 and traveled to San Francisco. His brothers joined the many prospectors who were after gold, but James decided to go to work at The Pioneer Steam Coffee and Spice Mills. The end of the Civil War saw a downturn in the economy that impacted many businesses but allowed Folger, who had become a partner, to buy out all the other partners and establish J.A. Folger & Co.

Over the next three decades, his company flourished amidst the strong presence of coffee importers in San Francisco. This group was the first to adopt a revolutionary methodology for making purchase decisions. Where the common practice for hundreds of years had been to judge green coffee visually, looking for characteristics showing consistency, good color, lack of defects, size, and so on, Folger and his peers began to cup-test their shipments. Testing each shipment for taste meant roasting a small batch of every load and tasting it for its attributes. The process was far more cumbersome, but it proved to be a solid methodology that has continued globally to this day.

Folger died when he was only 54, and his son James A. Folger II took over the family business. He recalled a letter from his father that said that profitability of a business always came second to that business having a good reputation. Quality and reputation became key attributes among the best coffee companies over the next 170 years.

Chase and Sanborn

Caleb Chase and James Solomon Sanborn established Chase & Sanborn Coffee in 1878. Among a handful of young American entrepreneurs on the West and East Coasts, their Boston-based venture claimed to be the first to pack and ship fresh-roasted coffee in tins. Figure 13-1 shows the company's building in Boston.

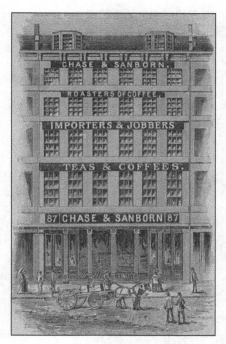

FIGURE 13-1:
Illustration of the
Chase & Sanborn
building at 87
Broad St., Boston,
Massachusetts.

Chase and Sanborn created quite an empire in the late 1800s, opening offices in both Chicago and Montreal, and by 1880 they were believed to have more than 25,000 local selling agents across the United States and Canada.

They were the first to see the potential of aggressive marketing (as shown in Figure 13-2), and not only did they spend considerable amounts of money on giveaway magazines and booklets that carried their brand to consumers, but they also outfitted delivery trucks with decorative, giant, green coffee coffeepots to catch the eyes of folks passing by their horse-drawn delivery vehicles.

Cup-testing, or cupping, was also part of their approach to purchasing green coffee, and as a result, their brand espoused both quality and a large and loud marketing about that quality to potential consumers.

FIGURE 13-2:
Chase & Sanborn
marketing
advertisement.

The Italians and Their Coffee Heritage

Innovators in coffee heading in one direction to create large quantities of brewed coffee stumbled on an idea that led to a start of an entirely new way to brew, and espresso was born. Here are some of those Italians.

Angelo Moriondo

On May 16, 1884, Angelo Moriondo filed a patent in Turin, Italy, for a steam machine that would instantly create coffee. This machine (Figure 13-3 shows the patent) was an early step toward espresso as it's known today because it brewed large quantities of coffee by introducing steam and water into grounds.

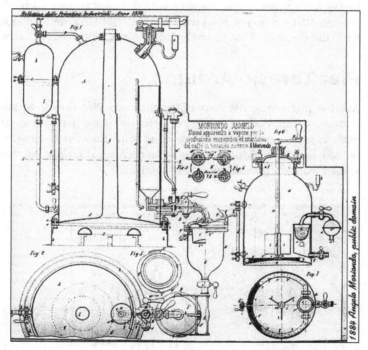

FIGURE 13-3:
Moriondo's
patent for a
steam-powered
coffee machine.

Source: www.wordpress.com

This idea for brewing would inspire the next wave of innovation, which would result in true espresso. Refer to Chapter 12 for more details.

Luigi Bezzera

Luigi Bezzera is known as the father of espresso. He invented the first machine that forced hot water, under pressure, through a small, compacted dose of finely ground, dark-roast coffee, in a short (25 to 35 seconds) amount of time.

His intent was to speed up the process of brewing so that his manufacturing company workers would shorten the time spent on their breaks. The downside of this quest for speed turned out to be a decidedly bitter brew.

Desiderio Pavoni

Desiderio Pavoni took the next visionary steps by purchasing Bezzera's patent and exploring variations of temperature and pressure to see if the taste could be made better. After a lot of experimenting with different recipes, he finally found one that worked: Water at 195 degrees with 8–9 BAR (*BAR* is a metric measurement of pressure) did the trick. That general guideline has continued for more than 100 years.

Pier Teresio Arduino

Another pioneering visionary of the time was Pier Teresio Arduino, who founded Victoria Arduino (see Figure 13-4), the company that would do more to spread early espresso culture than any other with its advertisements and philosophy behind the drink. Espresso was a modern creation and advertisements helped spread word of this cool new coffee culture.

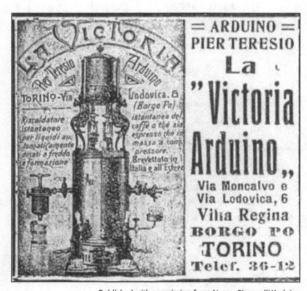

FIGURE 13-4:
Victoria Arduino
image.

Published with permission from Nuova Simonelli/Arduino

Making Waves in the United States

These folks all played a part and continue to be part of that enormous shift of coffee in the second and third waves. Here is a quick overview of the waves:

>> **First wave:** The first wave starts in the 1800s and lasted until the late 1900s. The focus is more on coffee as a product with coffee farms viewed as manufacturing factories. Although coffee companies marketed convenience, they sold lower grade commodity grade coffee. They used words like *gourmet* or *premium*, but they didn't substantiate what those words meant.

>> **Second wave:** This wave happens in the late 1900s when Peets Coffee, Tea & Spices and Starbucks introduce the idea of taste, quality, café experiences, and passionate service. The roaster as the craftsman was central to their efforts, and dark roast was the predominant offering.

>> **Third wave:** This wave occurs in the 1980s and 1990s. This wave sees the beginning of recognition for special coffees and the Specialty Coffee Association of America. (The Specialty Coffee Association of America merged with the global Society Coffee Association in 2017.) Global interest in roasting and brewing spread to Europe, Scandinavia, and Australia. In the late 1990s Trish Rothgeb first uses the actual term "third wave." (Refer to the later section, "Trish Rothgeb" for more details.)

Alfred Peet

Chapter 4 acknowledges Alfred Peet's contributions to coffee as the son of a coffee roaster. However, his love for the smell and taste of coffee spurred him to provide consumers with coffee that was significantly better than what they were accustomed to. His small coffee shop, Peets Coffee, Tea & Spices, in San Francisco (now one of the most respected coffee businesses and owned by JDE Peets and a part of the JAB family of businesses) became the birthplace of *specialty coffee* (coffee prized for its flavor qualities; see Chapter 4 for more details about specialty coffee).

Peet's journey wasn't easy. His childhood was marked by a controlling father, Peet's poor performance in school, and the experience of growing up in wartime Europe. Despite these challenges, he developed a love for coffee and the world it would open for him.

In 1948, after working for his father as an apprentice for ten years, Peet set out on a trip that took him to Indonesia, New Zealand, and eventually San Francisco. He had solid experience and landed a job with one of the San Francisco importing companies that worked with the big roasters. It was that experience and losing his job with a coffee importer in 1965 that solidified his vision that there was an opportunity in increasingly affluent America to provide consumers with coffee that was significantly better than what was then available.

Erna Knutson

As a coffee buyer, Erna Knutson is known for her uncompromisingly high standards. She's played an integral role in the growth of specialty coffee and is a founder of the Specialty Coffee Association of America (SCAA).

Her beginnings in the coffee industry were humble. She started as a secretary for a San Francisco coffee and spice importer. While doing the clerical work of tracking incoming and outgoing coffees, Knutson was asked by her boss to try to sell small quantities of partial lots (less than a full container) of green Arabica beans.

A few small roasting businesses were starting up in the 1970s (refer to Chapter 4 for more on their history), and their interest in better-quality green Arabica beans, combined with her entry into the sellers' market, enabled her to get a start.

Although Knutson had no expertise to speak of, she was aggressive about learning and spent any time she could in the cupping room, tasting with the less-than-supportive men who were obliged to give her entrée into their cloistered world. High-quality coffee now had a legitimate supply chain, and a woman had broken through in a clearly male-dominated world.

ALFRED PEET — HIS REVERENCE FOR COFFEE

One of my greatest memories was an opportunity to cup-taste coffee with Peet in the early 2000s. My work at the time involved coffee education, and my boss, Scott McMartin, had developed a friendship with Peet that led to my invitation to join them to taste a few coffees.

I was nervous, and my nerves weren't calmed by Peet's brusque demeanor and the seriousness of his approach. We tasted across a few growing regions, with coffees from Colombia, Guatemala, and Kenya, and finished the lineup with some darker French and Italian roast samples.

He said little until we had all finished, and then rapidly ran down the lineup with his thoughts about each coffee. While observing him, I realized he enjoyed a true camaraderie with the group that had joined him and that he was a true hero of the industry in which we all worked. The common denominator was that we all loved coffee.

Over the next 20 years, Knutson played an integral role in the growth of what is now known as specialty coffee. In fact, she was the first to use that term when she was quoted in an interview in 1974 in the *Tea & Coffee Trade Journal*.

In 1991 the SCAA recognized her as the first recipient of their SCAA Lifetime Achievement Award. She was honored by the SCAA again in 2014 when she was celebrated as a founder of the SCAA.

ON THE WEB

Check out www.youtube.com/watch?v=ibxnQBaTMoU to watch her acceptance speech from 2014.

George Howell

My first coffee mentor, George Howell has become a legend in coffee today. I remember him as a generous, passionate, wildly knowledgeable, and opinionated host at the original Coffee Connection, where he shared French press–brewed coffees from around the world with amazing stories and dreams for the future of coffee.

He and his wife Laurie arrived in Boston in 1974. They had lived in the San Francisco area for the six years leading up to that coastal move and were accustomed to having access to some really good coffees. That wasn't the case in Boston in 1974. Although George's studies had been in art and literature and he had been a gallery owner in California, he envisioned an opportunity to bring all he loved together into a coffeehouse.

The Howells, along with their partner Michael DaSilva, opened the Coffee Connection in a hip, new shopping space fashioned from a parking garage. They purchased their coffee from Erna Knutson.

The Coffee Connection wasn't a secret for long, as students and more and more suburban coffee lovers found their way to the familiar bean bar with its low-stooled counter.

Through the wonderfully informative, highly caffeinated public tasting seminars that Howell hosted at the Coffee Connection roasting facility — located next door to the Boston Design Center on the old waterfront — and singularly generous, focused, one-to-one coffee conversations at the counter of the shop, he solidified his reputation. I was a frequent attendee and beneficiary of both.

Over the next 20 years, Howell and the Coffee Connection expanded to 24 stores, and throughout New England were respected as *the* place, with *the* top coffee people in their baristas and roasters when it came to coffee. In 1994, he sold the Coffee Connection to Starbucks. In 1996, he received a Lifetime Achievement Award from the SCAA.

Free to begin exploring, Howell traveled extensively over the next few years, and in 1997 was engaged by the United Nations and International Coffee Organization to work on models of economic sustainability for coffee farmers. In 1999, he joined colleagues in the industry to establish the Cup of Excellence program, a competition and auction designed to help farmers receive more money for their high-quality coffee.

ON THE WEB

Now back in the retail business with George Howell Coffee (www.georgehowell coffee.com), Howell continues to provide inspiration as a generous educator, aficionado, and respected coffee connoisseur.

Howard Schultz

No matter what you think about Starbucks, one thing is clear: Howard Schultz is the mastermind behind the omnipresent coffee company. He combined a love for coffee and a love for community, with Starbucks being the end result.

The first of his family to graduate from college, he began his working life with an indelible impression of what it was like to grow up poor. In his first book, *Pour Your Heart Into It: How Starbucks Built a Company One Cup at a Time,* he shares a memory about his dad being out of work as a result of an injury and the subsequent ordeal the family went through. He acknowledges that childhood experience as a driving inspiration to do something different on behalf of people if the situation ever arose in which he had the power or position to do so. That focus on people would be central to many efforts and ideas Starbucks pursued and still pursues today. Perhaps none was more important or is recounted with greater pride by him than the day in 1991 Starbucks began offering *stock options* — a piece of ownership in the company called "Bean Stock" — to every employee, even those working part-time (more than 20 hours per week).

An unlikely unfolding of experiences in the late 1970s and early 1980s led Schultz, a Brooklyn native and young sales representative for a European housewares company, to travel to Seattle to see one of his accounts, Starbucks Coffee, Tea & Spices. At the time, Starbucks was a small, dry goods purveyor, owned by three young entrepreneurs in Seattle's Pike Place Market, but the visit sparked an emotional response and inspiration in Schultz.

He recognized something special in what was happening in that small shop, and not long after, he and his family moved to Seattle where he took on the role of the company's marketing head. Keep in mind that in 1983, the number of roasters throughout the United States who were selling specialty coffee was miniscule: the one Starbucks in Seattle, Peet's in San Francisco, Coffee Connection in Boston, Zabars in New York City, and a few others.

HOWARD SCHULTZ — AN AUTHENTIC, PASSIONATE, CREATIVE, VISIONARY COFFEE GUY

In February 1995, I left a 19-year teaching career to join Starbucks as a barista. In the fall of 1996, on the first day that my promotion to store manager was official, I met Howard Schultz.

I vividly recall sharing my career experience and remember that he listened with a focus that was almost unnerving. A few hours later, as he and his entourage were leaving, he stopped and began walking over to a group of us who were standing by the entrance. He walked right up to me and thanked me for taking the time to tell him my story.

I spent the next 25 years working at Starbucks in several roles. While my work intersected occasionally with him as the CEO, we weren't peers. I did however enjoy (most of the time, as his directness and capacity to make decisions quickly could be frightening!) opportunities to engage and collaborate, and I always understood he was interested in me and the work I was doing, a feeling I'm confident was celebrated by many other *partners* (what Starbucks employees are called) then and right up to his retirement from the company.

Chapter 4 discusses in greater detail how Schultz had a dream of combining coffee, cafés, and community in one place and how Starbucks took off.

Mary Williams

Mary Williams is a pioneer in the coffee industry — one (like many) in which women haven't had an easy path. Her career spanned more than 30 years, and in that time her work as a buyer led her to almost every country covered in Chapters 6, 7, and 8, where she was responsible for more than buying great green coffee. What she's known best for is that she identified the need for sustainability efforts with growers and processors well before these efforts were seen as fundamental.

Williams was working in San Francisco when the Starbucks team recruited her as a buyer in 1993. Growth was the keyword, and Williams was charged with establishing and maintaining a pipeline of high-quality, green coffee in quantities that were constantly being revised upward. During that time, she set a high standard for quality and also took her burgeoning relationships with growers and processors beyond the basic transaction to sustainability efforts. Her work on behalf of the environment and also the lives of the farmers, processors, and their families established many of the sourcing practices that are now admired today, more than 25 years after Williams introduced them.

Both the Rainforest Alliance and the SCAA recognized her for her lifetime achievement in specialty coffee.

David Schomer

Perhaps no one has exerted a quieter but more monumental influence over coffee, specifically espresso, than David Schomer. In 1988 he and Geneva Sullivan opened Vivace. Both left technical, non-coffee jobs to man Vivace's first operation, a coffee cart in downtown Seattle.

Now, more than 30 years later, he has established himself as a true legend of coffee, having made popular and ubiquitous the practice of latte art and the Vivace signature rosetta, as well as having written some of the most widely read and respected books on espresso. I highlight a visit to Vivace in Chapter 16.

Ted Lingle

Another of the unsung heroes of specialty coffee, Ted Lingle impacted the industry through two significant contributions. He wrote two important books and served as executive director of the SCAA for 15 years. His legacy touches the lives of every barista and every member of the global coffee community.

Lingle spent the first 20 years of his coffee career as vice president of marketing for Lingle Bros. Coffee, Inc., a business started by his grandfather in 1920 in Los Angeles.

In 1985, he wrote the *Coffee Cuppers' Handbook: A Systematic Guide to the Sensory Evaluation of Coffee's Flavor,* and in 1995, he followed up with *The Coffee Brewing Handbook: A Systematic Guide to Coffee Preparation.* These two are essential books for café and at-home baristas.

He also served on the board of the National Coffee Service Association and was elected an honorary member in 1990. He was one of the founding co-chairmen of the SCAA. In 1991, Lingle was appointed executive director of the SCAA, a position he served in for 15 years. In 2006, Lingle retired from the SCAA to become the new executive director for the Coffee Quality Institute (CQI). He stepped down from this position in 2013, but currently serves as CQI's senior advisor.

Trish Rothgeb

Over 25 years in coffee has afforded Trish Rothgeb some extraordinary opportunities in coffee. She has taken advantage of them to establish herself as an inspiring icon and voice in the industry.

Chapter 4 mentions Rothgeb as being attributed with naming the waves of development in the specialty coffee industry. For consumers today, including myself, who identify as part of the current wave — a fourth, or continuation of the third as coined by Rothgeb — it's relevant to understand that the idea was derived from an aspiration to achieve more. Rothgeb is a pioneer and role model because she has done just that.

Rothgeb was co-founder and owner of San Francisco's Wrecking Ball Coffee Roasters. She served on the executive council of the Roasters Guild for the SCAA, was on the board of directors of the World Barista Championship, and was a founding member of the Barista Guild of America.

As director of programs for quality and educational services at the CQI, she continues in a role where she influences the entire industry in positive and impactful ways.

Nick Cho

Another overlooked but important groundbreaking coffee personality is Nick Cho. Co-founder of Wrecking Ball Coffee Roasters, and later, founder of Murky Coffee in 2002, Nick has maintained a presence in the industry over the past two decades as a critical voice, innovator, and advocate for the barista.

ON THE WEB

Check out this terrific interview of Nick Cho on www.sprudge.com. Just search "Episode Three Nick Cho cascara."

Examining Café Culture, Espresso, and Competitions

An almost secret world exists that is all about cafés, competitions, and the unique people who drive the coffee community to be a special one. Who is that genuine and exuberant guy in the hat who seems to be everywhere at barista competitions, who makes tampers, invented the best, cutting-edge coffee scale? Read on to meet them and a few others I admire.

Gianni Cassatini

Sporting his trademark Borsalino fedora, Gianni Cassatini seems to be everywhere, and everyone seems to know him. Cassatini was born in 1937 and worked with the Simonelli group for 40 years. He's a true ambassador of the unique coffee family, the community of coffee that gathers most often for competitions.

Watch a livestream of a global coffee competition and look beyond the stage at the audience. You'll likely see him standing proudly, as competitors, many years his junior, demonstrate their craft for the judges. When they're done, he's often the first to high-five or hug them as they clear the stage. His smile is infectious, and the generosity of his spirit unlimited and 100-percent genuine.

Reg Barber

Although Reg Barber rarely stood directly in the limelight during his 30 years in the coffee industry, he made sure that coffee industry champions appeared in the public eye. Not only were Reg Barber Enterprises the manufacturers of the coffee competition's biggest awards, but they also made the tampers preferred by dozens of competitors and baristas around the globe.

The familiar RB logo, inlaid in hand-turned wood, often topped the familiar steel or aluminum base, but the variety was endless. His tamper design was the first to incorporate separate, attachable tops and bottoms. It truly was a revolutionary design that changed the espresso industry.

Rex Tseng and Aaron Takao Fujiki

As an unheralded pioneer, Rex Tseng introduced an innovation that seemed so sensible that it was a wonder it hadn't happened sooner. In collaboration with designer Aaron Takao Fujiki, he created the Acaia Pearl scale.

I learned early in my coffee brewing explorations that following the recipe was key. Two tablespoon scoops was the standard measure, and most of us in the biz had a collection of utensils for volumetric measure. I recall reading in the early 2000s that some brewers had begun to use kitchen scales to achieve more precision and consistency.

In 2013 Fujiki designed a most beautiful piece, and Tseng, through his multigeneration, family-owned, precision-scale company, delivered the Acaia Pearl scale. Together, they infused their invention with highly sophisticated style and innovative features.

Andrew Milstead

Innovating in an existing and established business space takes a special vision and drive, and Andrew Milstead has both of those. The idea of a coffee shop wasn't new, but stepping in as an experienced roaster and choosing to curate other roasters' coffees into a new concept was a game changer, and Andrew was among the first to break that new ground.

Andrew Milstead celebrates an anniversary on September 13, and many of us in the coffee industry celebrate along with him, because that was the day, in 2011, that Milstead & Co. opened in Seattle. Milstead worked in a few places in coffee before he finally landed in the Pacific Northwest.

Originally from Maryland, he attained his first job in the industry with Dunn Brothers Coffee in Minneapolis, where he worked his way up to a roaster position. It was there that he helped open a multi-roaster coffee bar, a concept that would stay with him over the next few years, as he spent time as both a barista and a barista competitor.

In 2009 he moved to Seattle and made opening his own shop his primary focus. Still intrigued by the novel idea of the multi-roaster approach, rather than pursuing roasting himself, he created a well-thought-out business plan for his own café.

Milstead & Co. garnered immediate recognition in the Seattle coffee scene, and it wasn't long before he and his team received national attention for his multi-roaster concept and for their professionalism, innovative approach, and simply delicious output.

James Hoffmann

Recognized as the world's first barista champion, James Hoffmann also has positioned himself as a passionate, trend-setting leader in the advancement of global specialty coffee through his work in the United Kingdom.

Being the top barista in the world may seem a monumental accomplishment, and it certainly is; however, Hoffmann understands the voice he gained by winning the title, particularly given the technological advancements all consumers and coffee lovers have experienced through the growth of social networking.

ON THE WEB

Hoffmann's website (www.jameshoffmann.co.uk/) is an excellent place to begin if you want to understand the extensive contributions he has made in the nearly 20 years that he has been part of the specialty coffee industry. Since his earliest days as a barista in 2003, Hoffmann has shared his passion for coffee and a compassion for its people throughout the supply chain.

Furthermore, he has authored multiple, well-respected books about coffee and is a sought-after voice of the industry when it comes to new equipment to brew, cutting-edge accessories, and education that advances the barista's craft.

Perhaps nowhere has he made a larger impact than through his YouTube channel. Just go to www.youtube.com and search for "James Hoffman." There he has more than 500,000 followers and hosts the show regularly on a broad series of coffee topics, with a wonderfully personal, humble, and insightful presence. A community builder extraordinaire, on September 21, 2019, Hoffmann hosted the world's largest cupping event, and on October 3, 2020, he hosted the world's largest tasting event.

Matt Perger

Matt Perger, who hails from Australia, is another former championship-caliber competitor who leveraged his accomplishments in a huge way on the global coffee front.

He has racked up several awards, including the following:

>> The 2012 World Brewers Cup

>> Titles from the Australasian Specialty Coffee Association (AASCA) and the Detpak Australian Barista Championship

>> Third place at the 2011 World Barista Championship

>> Second place in the 2013 World Barista Championship

Working in support of his personal vision of making coffee better, Perger created Barista Hustle (www.baristahustle.com), perhaps the most comprehensive, professional-level, online coffee curriculum available today. Chapter 14 discusses Barista Hustle more.

Colin Harmon

Originally from Dublin, Colin Harmon is another global competitor who has established a voice and worked to advance the industry.

He realized in 2008 that a career as an investment fund professional was inconsistent with his burgeoning passion for coffee. He started as an entry-level barista at Coffee Angel, a Dublin shop, and aggressively indulged his passion. Not only did he place fourth at the World Barista Championship in 2009, but he also won the Irish Barista Championship four times.

Colin currently runs 3fe Coffee (`https://3fe.com/`). His most recent contribution to the industry was his book, *What I Know About Running Coffee Shops*.

Ryan Soeder

From his start as a Starbucks barista in Louisville, Kentucky, to stints with Counter Culture, Intelligentsia, and Sunergos Coffee, where he was head of quality control, training, and coffee education, Ryan Soeder has fearlessly shared his uncompromising passion for quality and heartfelt commitment to the relevance and specialness of the barista role.

He is a celebrated barista competitor and latte art champion and has authored the book, *Barista Secrets: Creative Coffee at Home*. His online training videos are recognized globally. If a barista has served you a milk-based espresso beverage, then more than likely, he has used Soeder's videos as a learning tool.

Andrea Allen

Perhaps one of the most moving experiences I've had in coffee was to witness Andrea Allen in her competition presentation for the 2017 U.S. Barista Championship. Like many in the industry, I've always followed the competitions, and I was aware that 2017 was Allen's fourth consecutive year of competition, which isn't unusual; many competitors commit to a few years of involvement in the hopes that they'll be crowned champion.

What she did that year in competition was revolutionary and established her as a multi-faceted, innovative, and insightful pioneer in specialty coffee.

For the uninitiated, I can explain that the competitions essentially involve a timed stage presentation where skilled and articulate baristas demonstrate their skill using an espresso machine and grinder, a special coffee or coffees, and various additional professional tools (often some that are brand new to the industry). They present an espresso course, a milk beverage course, and a signature beverage of their creation. The highlights are the coffee, the technology, and the barista's message, not necessarily in that order.

What stood out for me was her focus on the human elements beyond the coffee story and the technology. She moved the judges and audience, generating an emotional response that I'd never seen before in a competition. She came in second that year.

She returned to the competition over the next three years and earned first place in 2020. Allen became the second female-identifying competitor within two years to take the title. Her message was clear: to show kindness toward others, to be responsible for how people treat each other, to build community, and to be generous in sharing what people have. Couple that with some amazing coffees, including the species, Eugenioides, which was blended in the portafilter with a second coffee before extraction, and the use of a mirror and an almost blind tasting by the judges to finish. (See the nearby sidebar for more information.)

Allen has used her voice in support of women, baristas, and the industry for almost a decade now and has been inspiring industry leaders. She owns Arkansas-based Onyx Coffee Lab with her husband, where their mantra is "never settle for good enough."

A BIT MORE ABOUT EUGENIOIDES

Colombia Inmaculada Eugenioides is considered to be one of the parents of modern Arabica coffee. *Eugenioides* is a very difficult coffee to grow, yielding only 150 grams per tree of unmilled coffee. It contains about half the caffeine of Arabica coffee, which causes it to have almost no bitterness. The defining characteristic of this coffee is its almost unbelievable sweetness. It has a compelling lack of citric acidity that we so often experience in coffee.

As I share in Chapter 2, *Coffea Arabica* is the species that has become synonymous with specialty coffee. More than 100 species of *Coffea* have been described, and *Eugenioides* is hailed as a progenitor of modern Arabica.

IN THIS CHAPTER

» **Whipping up a coffeehouse cup of coffee at home**

» **Making espresso at home**

» **Drinking great coffee away from your home**

» **Tapping into other resources for more about coffee**

» **Predicting what the future holds**

Chapter **14**

Looking at Where Coffee Is Today

There has never been a better time to be a coffee consumer than today. Despite ongoing political and economic turmoil and a true threat from climate change to name just a few significant issues, coffee continues to be grown, processed, transported, roasted, packaged, brewed, and sold.

In this chapter I put on my consumer hat and give you things to think about as you explore beans and brewing at home. Coffee choices and gear are key to preparing coffee at home, and you may be surprised at the endless array of choices you have.

I've always been an involved and curious consumer of coffee. Here I share some thoughts about thinking beyond what I'm tasting, to the other aspects of the coffee consumer experience that make me feel good while I'm enjoying great coffee. I hope you get a taste for my excitement.

I find an adage among many coffee aficionados to be inspiring: You and I can never know everything there is to know when it comes to coffee. As the world continues to change, every consumer has access to immeasurable opportunities to learn. Here I share some of my favorite resources about coffee and some new ones I'm itching to dig in to.

THE BEANS IN THE BEGINNING

Prior to the early 1970s, coffee was pretty simple. Sadly, most of what was available was pretty bad as well. You could go to your grocer, and the choice was between brands of ground, canned coffee, or whole bean. The whole bean was often displayed in open containers ready to be scooped, or in clear plastic dispensers.

Consumers were particularly enthusiastic at the time about instant varieties, as marketing gurus touted the latest technological innovations that made theirs not only the easiest but also the best tasting.

Today that same grocery experience has been markedly improved, and your available options range from some that haven't changed much in 50 years, to some that offer a chance to experience the best of what is out there today in more modern ways thanks to the Internet and probably in more spots in your own neighborhood thanks to the proliferation of terrific small coffee shops all over the world.

Brewing Coffee at Home

When brewing coffee at home, you have a multitude of choices. The following sections focus on the beans, as well as the equipment you need to brew at home.

Finding coffee today

Today, many varieties of coffees are available if you want to brew at home. Beyond grocery and convenience stores, coffeehouses like Starbucks or your local coffee shop are eager to get your coffee-for-home business. Of course, with the growth of online trade, you can also look well beyond your neighborhood to secure coffees to brew.

During the first six months of the stay-at-home quarantine in response to the COVID-19 pandemic of 2020, I secured some amazing coffees from sources and roasters all over the world. Prices were wide-ranging as I indulged my curiosity and desire to experience and explore.

Here is a list from that brief window of time. It includes a few of my favorite roasters, and some that I had never tried before. Remember that this list is far from exhaustive. You can connect with thousands of roasters both in your home town and thanks to the Internet. These are just a few of my recommendations and some coffees I've enjoyed from them in the past few months:

>> **Tim Wendelboe** (www.timwendelboe.no/my-subscription)

Finca Tamana, Caturra and Variedad Colombia, producer Elias Roa

Warenew, SL28 & Ruiru11, produced by smallholder farms Embu, Kenya

>> **Onyx Coffee Lab,** Rogers, Arkansas (https://onyxcoffeelab.com/)

Colombia Eugenoides, Las Nubes Farm

Costa Rica Las Lajas Natural

Costa Rica las Lajas Honey

Kenya Gachatha OT-18

Colombia La Pirámide, Typica, Caturra

Panama Elida Estate Anerobic

Colombia Gesha, Inmaculada Concepcion Farm

>> **JBC Coffee Roasters,** Madison, Wisconsin (www.jbccoffeeroasters.com/)

Twisted V.5 Espresso, Africa, Central America, Sumatra

>> **Stamp Act Coffee,** Seattle, Washington (https://stampactcoffee.com/)

Harsu Haro, Guji Ethiopia

>> **Camber Coffee,** Bellingham, Washington (https://cambercoffee.com)

Colombia Palomas Del Sur

>> **Milstead & Co. Blend** (www.milsteadandco.com)

Kenya Gakuyuini AA, Kirinyaga SL-28, SL-34, Ruiru11

Ethiopia Halo Beriti

>> **Ruby Colorful Coffees,** Nelsonville, Wisconsin (https://rubycoffee roasters.com)

San Sebastian Coatlan, Mexico

>> **Blue Bottle Coffee,** Oakland, California (https://bluebottlecoffee.com/)

Costa Rica Terrazu La Lia Black Honey Anerobic

Guatemala El Inerjo Ruby Gesha Natural

Fall Blend 2020

>> **Eccentricity Coffee Company,** Cleveland, Ohio (https://eccentricity coffee.com/)

Panama Lycello Blue, Washed Gesha

>> **Elemental Coffee Company,** Watertown, Massachusetts (https://elemental beverage.co/)

Snapchill George Howell, Montecarlos Estate, El Salvador

Snapchill George Howell, Nano Challa, Jimma, Ethiopia

Snapchill Little Wolf Roasters, Ipswich Massachusetts, Companion Blend

Keeping it fresh

The roaster has transformed the coffee bean into something that can be ground and brewed. After all, coffee is not only an ingredient in your recipe for a drink, but it's also a perishable product. Hence, it needs to be carefully treated like any fresh product, and it's subject to deterioration just like other fresh foods and ingredients are.

Protecting your beans

The enemies of freshness are air, light, heat, and moisture (see Chapter 10, where I discuss them in greater detail). Consumers depend on roasters to package and protect their beans. Those bags of coffee you see on the shelves represent some marvelous technological advancements, both in the actual material they're made of, and in the way they are sealed.

Add a special valve design that is almost ubiquitous in coffee packaging today, and the result is a perfect storage container for coffee. I also keep my coffee in a cool, dry, dark cupboard.

Thinking a bit differently

One additional caveat: Coffee that has just been roasted, seemingly the freshest of all, isn't ready to enjoy fully until it has gone through a couple of days of *degassing* (giving off carbon dioxide, or CO_2). The science behind this involves the CO_2 from the coffee's former life as a plant that causes it to actually repel water during the brewing if it's still too fresh. You get a bitter taste that won't show up if you just wait a few days for the coffee to go through the degassing.

WARNING

Steer clear of the glass- or plastic-displayed coffee dispensers often seen in grocery stores and away from grinding your own in those same stores, unless you're confident that they have paid attention to freshness, cleanliness, and maintenance. Roasted coffee oils are notoriously difficult to remove, and if they collect on those dispensers, there is a good likelihood that some rancid oil will connect with any fresh coffee that you add, and the taste of coffee from there will surely be affected.

Making use of some new and exciting gear

Here are some apparatus and gear that you can incorporate into your at-home brewing.

Brewers

Brewers are the devices you use to bring the coffee and hot water together and keep them in contact to expedite correct extraction and create good-tasting coffee. Some of the gear is really basic and inexpensive, some is technologically complex, making work on your end simpler, and some is complex, leaving much of the decision-making and action to you as a brewer. Refer to Chapter 11 for more about the basics of brewing, including pour-over brewing, immersion, and a few variations. If you want to brew your coffee at home, the following sections discuss some of the most popular brewing methods you can try.

HAND BREWING

Melitta-style hand-pour filter holders are ubiquitous and can vary greatly in terms of quality. The material they're constructed of (plastic, metal, or ceramic) and the interior design configuration, while seemingly unimportant, can play a crucial role in temperature consistency, bloom, circulation, flow, and eventual extraction results.

Here are two of the most widely used pour-over filter holders you can use at home when brewing coffee for friends or for yourself.

>> **Hario V-60** (www.hario-usa.com/)

>> **Kalita Wave** (www.kalita-usa.com/kalita-wave-brewing-guide/)

>> **Chemex** (www.chemexcoffeemaker.com)

I've used the first two, but I must admit that as a devoted hand brewer, my favorite brewing device is the Chemex. (Chapter 11 discusses this 1930s invention and its investors.) Refer to the nearby sidebar for more details.

AUTOMATIC BREWING

Many home brewers prioritize convenience and consistency and are willing to forgo handwork and craftsmanship. Automatic brewers were created with only those benefits in mind, but even so, some outstanding options are available.

THE PAST BECOMES COOL AGAIN

The Chemex brewer has popped up twice in my lifetime, and in the interim was all but lost as a relic of old-fashioned brewers and brewing.

My mom was a sophisticated consumer and chef in the 1950s during my childhood, and coffee was one of her passions. My earliest exposure to the Chemex, which in the 1950s had become a cool way to brew coffee for hip consumers, was looking up at my mom carefully pouring her water onto the grounds in her Chemex. I can still see the familiar and signature large paper flaps of the unique filter paper.

From the late 1950s until the early 2000s Chemex went out of style as other brewers eclipsed any interest in this "antique" apparatus. However, the young, entrepreneurial coffee afficionados of the third wave resurrected the brewer and interest in it exploded. What was old-fashioned became hip again.

The SCA certified these brewers as the best (and I completely agree):

>> Behmor Brazen Plus 2.0 Control Brew System

>> Bonavita BV1902DW 8-Cup One-Touch Coffee Maker

>> Braun MultiServe Coffee Machine

>> Breville BDC450 Precision Brewer Coffee Maker

>> Brim 8 Cup Pour Over Coffee Maker

>> BUNN HB Heat N Brew Programmable Coffee Maker

>> Cuisinart CPO-850 Coffee Brewer

>> Ninja CM407 Specialty Coffee Maker

>> Paderno 9-Cup Balanced-Brew Coffee Maker

>> Technivorm Moccamaster 59618 KBG Coffee Brewer

Of these my favorite is the Technivorm. I've recommended it dozens of times and never had anyone be anything but 100 percent pleased by the machine's simplicity, flexibility, and consistency. More importantly, they've been impressed with the quality of their finished brew.

Today, hundreds of automatic pour–over brewers are available. If you pick an SCA–certified coffee maker, remember that it won't brew quickly. Given the time and temperature requirements, brewing a great cup of coffee can easily take up to eight minutes.

BREWING A "GOLDEN CUP" OF COFFEE: THE SCA'S REQUIREMENTS

The Specialty Coffee Association (SCA) defines perfectly brewed coffee as the Golden Cup Standard. The SCA Golden Cup requirements for brewing coffee are as follows: Coffee shall exhibit a brew strength, measured in total dissolved solids, of 11.5 to 13.5 grams per liter, corresponding to 1.15 to 1.35 "percent" on the SCA Brewing Control Chart, resulting from a soluble extraction yield of 18 to 22 percent.

This recipe for success works best if paired with a great brewer, and the SCA provides an annual list of the brewers they have looked at and certified. Look for this SCA Brewer Certified Logo when shopping for a brewer for your home.

Some notable aspects of a Golden Cup of coffee are as follows:

- **Brewing temperature:** The ideal brewing temperature for coffee is 200°F ± 5°. So, the coffee maker should be able to heat water to 195–205°F and hold this temperature as the brewing begins. Although a lot of coffee makers heat water to this temperature, they can have trouble holding it as water is sent to the coffee grounds.

- **Time of water contact:** SCA-approved coffee makers should allow convenient contact time with coffee for ideal extraction, which depends on the coffee grind. To extract well, drip coffee makers usually work with medium grind and need 4 to 6 minutes. If you did use coarse grind, it can take up to 8 minutes to brew, whereas fine grind would need only 1 to 4 minutes.

- **Coffee quantity:** SCA recommends 1.63 grams of whole coffee beans per fluid ounce of water. When using ground coffee, that's roughly 55 grams for 34 ounces of water.

(continued)

(continued)

Refer to Chapter 11 for more discussion about important variables when brewing coffee.

If you're old enough, you may recall the Mr. Coffee brewer that was introduced in 1970. The idea was simple and launched a new wave of coffee brewing, which up until its introduction was dominated by percolator-style brewing. Sometimes also known as *cowboy coffee,* this percolator-style brewing incorporated the same hot water flowing over and over through the grinds. The result: The coffee was harsh and unpleasant compared to the Mr. Coffee.

CAPSULE OR POD BREWERS

Coffee pods and capsules have become prolific, and even though they were first inspired by simplicity, efficiency, and consistency, they have moved from poorly regarded compromises to substantially respected, high-quality options. Even coffee consumers who support the environment and who see the pods' and capsules' wasteful use of materials as suspect at best, can find companies that advocate recycling, reuse, and refilling.

There's no denying the popularity of this brewing technology and the proliferation of machine options and coffee varieties that are out there. I happily admit to having a small Nespresso machine in a spot in my kitchen and a sweet selection of Nespresso and Starbucks brand capsules in my cupboard.

Most days I fire up the pod machine for a quick taste while I prep my Chemex, Lido II, or Fellow Ode grinder, Acaia Pearl, and some whole bean for a second, more time-consuming brew.

Grinders

Somewhere along the way to your coffeemaker, the coffee must be ground to the correct particle size. If you purchase the beans online, buy beans that haven't been ground.

TIP

Although pre-shipment grinding is certainly convenient, you want to grind your coffee as close as possible to the time you're going to use it to brew. Pre-ground can still taste good when it's new, but after a few days, the flavor fades.

The options for a home grinder begin with the actual cutting or grinding part in the mechanism. There are two types:

- » **Blade grinders** are much less expensive and spin to chop up the coffee. It's possible to do an okay job of getting the correct particle size, although the results will be less consistent and less precise. The major issue with these grinders is that they heat up the coffee, and heat is an enemy of freshness and good-tasting results.

- » **Burr grinders** grind the coffee, and the consistency, efficiency (not heating up the particles), and often wide range of particle-size options make them a better choice, provided that one doesn't break your wallet. The best grinder is far more expensive than an average one.

You have a few solid options for home grinders, but I'm going to make a plug here for one brand. Thanks to a partnership, established in 1999 in the Pacific Northwest, between Kyle Anderson and Kyra Kennedy, Baratza Grinders were introduced. They've been the most regularly recommended grinders since then. They feature burr grinders with a choice between conical and flat burrs.

TECHNICAL STUFF

The burrs are grooved with tooth-like edges and are positioned inside the grinder to ensure that when the machine is turned on, their proximity is such that the beans are ground between them. Close together, they create fine particles, and further away, coarser particles. Both are a huge step up from the blade grinder, although they have some differences:

- » **Flat burr grinders** are thought to be a bit more precise, although they can heat up and are generally more expensive.

- » **Conical burr grinders** run quieter and cooler as they move the coffee vertically in the conical assembly.

ELECTRIC GRINDERS

Several electric models are available to help you grind your coffee at home:

- » Baratza Encore Burr Coffee Grinder

- » Baratza Virtuoso Conical Coffee Grinder

- » Bodum Bistro Burr Coffee Grinder

- » Cuisinart Supreme Grind Burr Mill

- » Fellow's Ode Brew Grinder

- » Krups Precision Burr Grinder

- » OXO BREW Conical Burr Coffee Grinder

HAND GRINDERS

In this age of automation, it's increasingly rare to see hand-driven accessories, but with coffee grinding, the legacy of the tool having begun that way hundreds of years ago has continued, and there are a couple that I highly recommend.

In my cabinet at home, I have the Orphan Espresso Lido II grinder (www.oehand grinders.com/). I have been using it for quite a few years, because space in my kitchen is at a premium (my wife is a chef, and we "negotiate" for counter space), and I prefer the quiet when I grind in the early morning. This grinder has steel, conical grinding burrs and a unique handle assembly that allows for smooth, efficient operation without too much manual effort. It has an extraordinarily simple grind-size adjustment feature and will grind in a full range from exceptionally fine to coarse.

Brewers who choose to grind by hand also praise these three choices:

>> Hario Skerton Plus Coffee Mill

>> Peugeot Bresil Coffee Mill

>> Porlex Mini Mill

Kettles

Hot water is a key element for your home brewing, and a kettle on a stovetop will get you water to brew with.

REMEMBER

If you drink water from your tap, you can probably use it to make very good coffee. If you don't like the qualities of your tap water, then that tap water will likely make disappointing coffee. Refer to Chapter 11 where I discuss water in greater detail.

As hand pouring gained attention in the third wave of coffee brewing, the Hario Buono kettle design became a fast favorite (see Figure 14-1). The comfortable handle, gooseneck pouring spout, and capacity (800 mL) are all ideal, and the kettle can be placed right on the stovetop for heating. The Hario Buono has an electric model as well.

If you want to equip your coffee spot at home with the most cutting-edge technology in gooseneck kettles, the one for you is the Fellow Brand, Stagg EKG. It's an electric kettle with a stunning design and variable temperature control, although I had to get used to the slower flow when I first switched from a Hario Buono to the Stagg. Both brands provide really great flow control.

OXO, Bonavita, and Brewista are other brands that offer gooseneck kettles.

FIGURE 14-1:
Hario Buono
kettle.

© Hario USA

Scales

Your coffee and water need to be measured if you want to follow a recipe and get consistently tasty results. A basic and oft-used solution is a simple scoop for the coffee, and a measuring cup for the water. The use of scales is another recent innovation.

You have a few options to choose from. I suggest the following:

>> **Acaia:** Founders Aaron Marcus and Rex Tseng were the first to introduce a stylish, precision, application-laden scale, and Acaia has become the most widely recognized brand globally. The Lunar model was designed with a waterproof setting for espresso functionality, where liquids might compromise the scale's circuitry. (Refer to Chapter 13 for more details.)

The Acaia Pearl model scale incorporated stellar design and features beyond anything that had been seen. Features as simple as timers and auto shut-off have given way to auto tare and fully programmable, individual brew-profile settings.

>> Brewista Smart Scale II

>> Hario V60 Coffee Drip Scale

>> Nourish Digital Coffee Scale

>> Pearl S model

>> Pyxis Ultralight

Making Espresso at Home

For a large segment of consumers, the idea of creating espresso beverages at home is a dream. The great news: You don't need to run a coffee shop to do it. Over the past decade or two, consumers have been able to purchase some amazing equipment and gear, so you can now match any café cup for cup with excellence. The following sections take a closer look at making espresso drinks in your home.

The machine

Central to espresso creation is a dedicated espresso machine with the capacity to pull shots at the correct pressure consistently and to steam milk. (Chapter 12 has more information about espresso machines.)

A home espresso machine is a significant investment, no matter where you start. As with any appliance, the costs, the possible extra investment in additional features, the brand integrity, and even the size (or footprint) are primary considerations, but they're just the first things you have to think about.

I've had countless conversations with folks who are interested in making their own espresso, and, in all honesty, my first inclination is to talk them out of doing full-scale brewing of espresso in their home kitchen. It's a big undertaking, particularly if you're accustomed to enjoying lattes and cappuccinos created by a professional barista at your local café.

Some great options are available, with a significant sector of the industry dedicated to making home espresso possible for everyone. The following three espresso machines are the most economical and attractive. They'd be hard pressed to stand up to the demands of a coffeehouse environment, but they're great to use at home:

>> Breville's Bambina Plus

>> Breville's Barista Touch

>> Gaggia's Classic Pro

If you want to elevate your game at home with espresso, you can look into buying one of the following three professional-grade home espresso machines:

>> La Marzocco's Linea Mini

>> Nuovo Simonelli's Musica

>> Slayer's Espresso Single Group

These three machines have many of the same criteria, features, and benefits, but because they all come from three of the most respected espresso machine manufacturers for cafés in the world, they're truly professional-caliber equipment, but sized and outfitted for a home setting.

The espresso grinder

You may want to purchase a grinder devoted to espresso. I offer a general discussion of grinders in the section, "Grinders," earlier in this chapter. As for grinding coffee devoted to espresso, here are some of my top suggestions:

>> Baratza Encore and Virtuoso grinders suit most home baristas.

>> Rancilio Rocky and Baratza Vario grinders offer a home barista even more precision, which can be key in creating the correct, finely ground coffee necessary for espresso.

Stepping Out — Drinking a Cup of Coffee Away from Home

The possibilities for coffee that exist after you leave home are seemingly endless and expanding all the time, as merchants of all kinds see the potential in including coffee in their customer experience. Coffee is present in so many places today:

>> **Coffeehouses:** You may think Starbucks is all there is to coffee. If so, you're missing out on a lot. Your neighborhood may have more to offer. Look at the countless cafés and coffee shops around your neighborhood, in your city, and in your travels for an extraordinary number where you can drink and appreciate coffee.

>> **Grocery stores, banks, auto dealers, and so on.** More and more places offer coffee to make their customers feel comfortable while they're doing business. Because of the ubiquity of superbly roasted beans and splendid high-tech brewing machines, the chances are surprisingly good that you'll find and enjoy a top-notch cup of coffee.

The experience of drinking a great cup coffee alone or with friends is enhanced with other variables as well, in particular, the human connection. I treasure a connection with coffee professionals, my baristas, when I travel away from home for coffee. That connection can make or break an experience for me and will figure profoundly in my decision to return to that place. For me, good taste becomes the gateway; the other variables, like being with friends and having a knowledgeable barista, support or diminish my positive feelings and the possibility of another visit.

THE VALUE PROPOSITION IS VITAL

I take very seriously a coffee company's value proposition, whether I'm drinking the company's coffee or buying and using its equipment. *Value proposition,* sometimes referred to as a *brand promise,* basically is a simple statement that captures the feeling the brand hopes to create for you.

I always want to be cognizant of that feeling and ask myself, "Is this purveyor doing the right things that go beyond simply providing me with a good coffee to either brew or drink? Or is this just a good product?"

With coffee, I think of the following in this order:

- The taste of the coffee, which relates to the quality of the coffee
- The price that is paid to the humans along the supply chain that help get the coffee to me
- The social factors, which refer to how the coffee relates to the lives of the people who grow and process it, and the lives of everyone along that supply chain
- The environmental elements that go into growing the coffee, moving it, roasting it, and eventually brewing it

You can find clues wherever you look today in your experiences with coffee. Perhaps a local barista who you speak with is proud about what she knows her company is doing in sourcing to enhance the quality of life for coffee farmers (see Chapter 2 for more information about sourcing).

After you gather a few facts about a coffee company, you can begin to establish your own researched impression by using some of the resources I share in this chapter.

Finding More Information about Coffee Today and in the Future

Whether you've established a home brewing setup or an espresso station (maybe even both!), or you're a dedicated customer and coffee connoisseur at your local coffeehouse — or most likely some combination of all three — your learning has begun. I bet you're at least wondering what possibilities exist in coffee to go to the next level. Fortunately, I have you covered. The following sections look at an array of online resources, podcasts, books, and magazines, and so much more to take your coffee experience to another level.

Focusing on the Specialty Coffee Association

At the top of my list for its heritage, credibility, breadth of content, and professionalism is the Specialty Coffee Association (SCA; https://sca.coffee/). Grounded in "openness, inclusivity, and the power of shared knowledge," the SCA membership is comprised of everyone from farmers to baristas. The SCA establishes standards and guidelines collaboratively and today maintains the most comprehensive and respected learning programs, as well as a constant flow of professional communications (professional papers, newsletters, podcasts, and more).

With four programs that focus on eight areas of study, the SCA offers the most professional-level curriculum, and for many participants this learning is part of their career development in a coffee role. It's open to everyone, though, and individual membership and basic-level classes are reasonably priced and offer an amazing depth of knowledge.

The Coffee Skills Program (CSP) offers these areas of study:

>> Introduction to coffee
>> Barista skills
>> Brewing
>> Green coffee
>> Sensory skills
>> Roasting

Add in a Coffee Sustainability program and a robust Coffee Technicians program, and you have it all covered with the SCA. Authorized SCA Trainers (AST), which I am one, teach classes all over the world.

Looking online

As a coffee-consuming citizen of the world, I have a part to play, and perhaps you're considering your role differently as you discover more about coffee.

A continued and sustained access to good-tasting coffee that is economically justified and produced in a socially and environmentally responsible way is important to me. I want to be informed enough to determine if the few dollars I contribute online, in a grocery or café, or with another purchase can have an impact, albeit a small one.

Go online and search for coffee-related resources. Here are some of my top choices:

>> **Sprudge** (`https://sprudge.com/`): I follow Sprudge to stay broadly connected. I met Zachary Carlsen and Jordan Michelman, who founded The Sprudge Report in 2009 (and which has since been renamed Sprudge). Based in Portland, Oregon, their blogging world has increased dramatically, and their online resource is a first stop for anyone looking for cutting-edge specialty coffee news. Virtually every city in the world that has some specialty-coffee cafés has had a look from a Sprudge reporter, and Sprudge's presence at international coffee competitions has made it an unrivaled source of up-to-date competition news as well.

>> **Barista Hustle** (`https://www.baristahustle.com`): Matt Perger is the creator and lead expert of the Barista Hustle. Matt and his team have created an amazingly comprehensive, well-constructed, and easy-to-use online platform that covers the full spectrum of what a barista or interested consumer might want to explore, including their Barista Hustle Unlimited Coffee Education Program.

>> **Starbucks Coffee Academy** (`https://starbuckscoffeeacademy.com`): Pleasant baristas with good coffee knowledge have always been an integral part of the Starbucks experience, but the content of Starbucks Barista training program was always for internal use only. With the recent introduction of the Starbucks Coffee Academy, all that changed, and consumers now have access to the entire program in the form of three levels of online classes. Also included are some beautiful assets, including images and films. This is a visually appealing, informative, user-friendly learning program that is well worth the time.

In addition, keep your eyes open for these three organizations for timely and insightful information about coffee that will assuredly enhance and inform your consumer experiences:

>> World Coffee Research (https://worldcoffeeresearch.org/)

>> Sustainable Coffee Challenge (www.sustaincoffee.org)

>> UC Davis Coffee Center (https://coffeecenter.ucdavis.edu/)

Listening to podcasts

Podcasting fills the airwaves, and your options are many. I highlight a couple of my favorites here:

>> **Keys to the Shop Podcast** (https://keystotheshop.com): I listen regularly to Chris Deferio's wide-ranging and insightful podcast. In fact, I was an honored guest on Episode 127 on March 7, 2019. The breadth of personalities and topics that he covers keeps me looking forward to what's coming next.

>> **Cat and Cloud Podcast** (https://catandcloud.com/pages/podcast): Jared Truby and Chris Baca host this podcast. As professional baristas with experience at every level of the specialty coffee business, they share their passion for coffee and compassion for the people in the business, while presenting a wonderful range of topics and personalities in their broadcasts.

You can find more coffee-related podcasts here (note that this list is far from complete):

>> Sourceress (https://www.sourceresshq.com/)

>> La Crema: Podcast de Café (https://soundcloud.com/lacremapodcast)

>> Specialty Coffee Association Podcast (https://soundcloud.com/specialtycoffee)

>> Craft Your Own Coffee Podcast (https://podcasts.apple.com/us/podcast/craft-your-own-coffee-podcast/id1473079080)

>> Boss Barista Podcast (http://bossbarista.com/homepage)

Perusing books and magazines

You can flip through hundreds of books and magazines as you explore more about coffee. Here are some books I've used in my career, and magazines I've received regularly to stay updated about what is happening in the world of coffee today:

>> ***The World Atlas of Coffee: From Beans to Brewing — Coffees Explored, Explained and Enjoyed,*** 2nd Edition, by James Hoffmann (Firefly Books): This book, the second edition of which was released in 2018, provides an in-depth opportunity to explore coffee thoroughly. In just a few years, this atlas has become a favorite reference for baristas and consumers. Check out Chapter 13 for more information.

>> ***Uncommon Grounds: The History of Coffee and How It Transformed Our World,*** by Mark Pendergrast (Basic Books): Out of all the resources I've used in my career, *Uncommon Grounds* has been the most valuable. The inspiration and importance of what has come before — the history of coffee, if you will — has always been central to my understanding and capacity to share. Pendergrast is an unrivaled storyteller and has helped me become a better one over the years.

   I've recommended *Uncommon Grounds* countless times to people who were curious about coffee, because its history reveals the scope and depth of the passion that humans have had for coffee, and this intense connection is matched only by a few other commodities in the world.

>> **Barista Magazine Online** (`www.baristamagazine.com`): This magazine, published in Portland, Oregon, has provided me with a connection to the world of the barista, the café, and coffee-growing origins that is genuine and grounding. For consumers, it offers a glimpse into the parts of the coffee world that are most connected to the experiences they're enjoying and are often unknown or misunderstood. Whether you frequently go to cafés or you're exploring coffee on your home front, this magazine offers inspiring, educational, and bona fide information about coffee.

>> ***Standart*** (`https://standartmag.com/`): Founded in 2015 by Michal Molcan, who is also the editor in chief, this magazine celebrates the beauty of the specialty coffee culture.

   A quarterly publication whose breadth, beauty, and intriguing vision have made it a cherished read of coffee lovers around the world, *Standart* was chosen by Sprudge readers as the coffee magazine of the year in 2017, 2018, and 2019. More than any other coffee magazine, *Standart* celebrates the humanity and beauty of specialty coffee while never compromising its credibility and always being a platform for the important voices in the word of coffee.

7

The Part of Tens

Chapter **15**

Ten (or So) Myths about Coffee Debunked

C offee is a staple around the world, served at different times of the day, depending on where you are. Despite its popularity, some myths about it still exist. This chapter debunks those commonly held myths so you can enjoy your next cup no matter.

Coffee Is Loaded with Caffeine

All coffee has caffeine except for decaffeinated coffee (which I discuss in detail in the section, "Decaf Coffee Isn't Real Coffee," later in this chapter). Although I prioritize my coffee-drinking decision-making so I can satisfy my insatiable curiosity and search for another coffee to put on my list of best ever, I can't deny that the energizing impact and increased alertness of caffeine remain a plus for me.

Coffee has general ranges of caffeine that are measured in mg (milligrams). Here are a few examples to give you an idea:

» Brewed coffee has about 95 mg in an 8-ounce serving.

» A single espresso (30g) has about 45 to 63 mg of caffeine.

>> A single shot latte has 45 to 63 mg.

>> A double shot latte has 90 to 126 mg.

Different types of beans or varietals (see Chapter 2) can have varying caffeine levels; the way they're roasted (see Chapters 9 and 10) and then brewed (see Chapter 11) can impact caffeine levels, but in the end the amount will still generally fall into the range I've shared.

Recent studies have found that most people can easily handle 100 to 200 mg — equivalent of one or two cups a day. Increasing consumption from 250 to 700 mg may bring on nausea, headaches, sleep difficulties, or increased anxieties. People who drink more than 1,000 mg of caffeine a day may experience heart palpitations.

Caffeine effects can last five to seven hours for most people, but be aware that generalizations only provide a starting point for your personal discovery as to how you react.

TIP

If you want an immensely entertaining experience, during which you can discover more about caffeine than you could imagine and live through one author's experience of going from coffee lover to cold-turkey abstinence in the name of research, hunker down with Michael Pollan's audiobook, *Caffeine: How Caffeine Created the Modern World* (Audible).

Coffee Has Tons of Calories

Coffee may well be the miracle diet beverage because it contains such few calories. Eight ounces of brewed coffee or an americano — my personal favorites — has less than 5 calories and a shot of espresso less than 3 calories. The calories can quickly escalate though if you add milk, cream, sugar, or syrups.

Statistics reveal that about 35 percent of coffee drinkers drink it *black*, that is without any milk, cream, sugar, and so on. However, the remaining 65 percent of coffee drinkers add extras to their coffee that significantly increase the calorie count.

Consider the following example: A tall, 12-ounce nonfat latte has about 100 calories, all coming from the nonfat milk. Add some vanilla syrup to create a vanilla, nonfat latte, and you're consuming around 150 calories. The calories can really add up, depending on how much syrup you add and how the syrup is made.

Coffee Is Bad for You

Depending on where you look in coffee's history, you can either substantiate or dispel this myth. I remember growing up in the 1950s and being told that coffee would stunt my growth. (My mom was generous and gave me some of hers with lots of cream and sugar anyways.)

Coffee has been thought to cause cancer, heart disease, stomach ulcers, exacerbate heart conditions, lead to an addiction to caffeine, and damage the digestive tract, which could lead to heartburn. Fortunately research has proven all these claims to be false.

The most recent and certainly brighter side of coffee's effects on health begins with studies that have made a correlation between type 2 diabetes risk and coffee versus non-coffee drinkers. According to researchers at the Aarhus University Hospital in Denmark, regular coffee drinkers have an 11 percent lower risk of developing the disease than non-coffee drinkers.

Additional research has shown that what once were thought to be heart and circulation risks now look to be benefits because coffee's effects on most people's blood vessels appear to be positive.

Furthermore, scientists are discovering every day about the antioxidant impact on oxidative damage and a link to cancer and have identified coffee is now a beneficial antioxidant-rich source with four important vitamins and minerals:

>> Riboflavin (vitamin B2)

>> Pantothenic acid (vitamin B5)

>> Manganese and potassium

>> Magnesium and niacin (vitamin B3)

WARNING Caffeine and the energy alertness benefits that coffee brings can be addictive, especially for some people. If your body reacts negatively to caffeine, you may need to significantly reduce it or even eliminate it. A complete withdrawal from coffee can be accompanied by headaches, irritability, and fatigue.

Decaf Coffee Isn't Real Coffee

Decaffeinated coffee begins its life just like any other coffee cherry on a tree in the earth somewhere in the Coffee Belt. (Chapter 5 discusses the Coffee Belt in greater detail.) The green coffee beans undergo the same processing and have the same flavor characteristics and key quality impacts as regular coffee. Decaffeinated coffee is coffee.

Coffee doesn't grow without caffeine, although there has been sporadic and yet to be successful research in the late 1900s and early 2000s to grow a coffee tree that yielded decaffeinated beans.

So what makes it decaf? The roasting company has the caffeine removed by a third party, that is, the caffeine is separated from the green, unroasted bean before the coffee arrives at the roasting and packing facility. When that element is removed, it carries the caffeine away with it. Refer to Chapter 10 for more details about decaffeination.

The caffeine captured is often sold to the soft drink or pharmaceutical industries for inclusion in some other products like aspirin or cola.

Instant Coffee Is Disgusting

A remarkably sizeable portion of the world's coffee consumers enjoy instant coffee. In fact, as recently as 2015 the estimate was that about 50 percent of coffee drinkers drank instant coffee. More than likely few of them would describe their experience as disgusting.

REMEMBER

Instant coffee is different in the following ways:

>> **Different type or quality of bean used:** The actual beans used for instant coffee may not always be Arabica. They may be Robusta or a combination of Arabica and Robusta. Taste may take a back seat to cost and availability. (Refer to Chapter 2 where I discuss the key qualities of green coffee.)

>> **Different approach to roasting:** Although the beans to make instant coffee have been roasted, the care and craftsmanship I highlight in Chapter 10 as part of the specialty coffee industry aren't a priority when making instant coffee.

Instant coffee has often been less desirable than ground coffee. That story began to change in late 2009 when Starbucks launched VIA Ready Brew. This product was the first to create an instant coffee that utilized Starbucks established sourcing practices, careful roasting, and the inclusion of a patented microgrind technology that helped maintain the coffee's taste, quality, and freshness. More recently companies like Sudden, Voila, Steeped, Dripkit, Copper Cow, and Swift have joined the instant coffee manufacturers that proudly offer products they believe match up to their non-instant counterparts.

Coffee Makers Only Need a Quick Rinse to Clean

When you and I brew coffee, we know that what we make is brown colored, sometimes a bit oily, with perhaps some ground particles that often make a big mess. Having to clean all that up is one of the reasons why instant coffee and capsules and pods have maintained and gained popularity. Making coffee can be messy!

After brewing a pot of coffee, you have all the gear, especially the filter holders, brewer carafes, and even the internal places that coffee moves in an automatic brewer that need more than a rinse.

Coffee oils are insidious and necessitate a bit of extra attention. I give my French press carafes or Chemex brewer a thorough warm water rinse right after I finish with them, and occasionally I put them aside to drain and dry without much more attention until the next time I use them. I also use good soap and water to wash them, which is much better than a rinse.

After a while you'll inevitably begin to see a need to clean them even more thoroughly than with soap and warm water. Residue, rancid coffee oils, and lime scale deposits may have formed on your brewing gear or inside your equipment. For the next level of cleanliness, I use a cleaner that comes in either powder or liquid; they're made to keep oils and mineral deposits at bay and are easy to use.

TIP

Every manufacturer offers guidance about descaling mineral buildup from the internal parts of a machine. Read the fine print of your automatic brewer or espresso machine instructions, which provide step-by-step instructions to descale coffee gear and will recommend you use vinegar or a specially made descaling solution.

All Coffee Tastes the Same

Although some younger or newer coffee drinkers acknowledge the names, bags, and countries on the coffee bags and labels are different, they often admit that when they begin tasting they can't really taste any difference.

I understand. When I was a barista in the 1990s, I worked in front of signs offering more than 23 whole bean coffees. Countries of origin, blends, and roast variations all contributed to the chaos, and my palate was overwhelmed. With some regular tasting and focused practice — which isn't difficult for any coffee lover — I discovered the different nuances of taste.

Check the chapters in Part 3 that examine how geographic range as well as the variety in green coffee through the growing, processing, and roasting result in an array of coffees with a diverse and varied taste.

The Coffee Industry Doesn't Have Any Innovation

Although many in the coffee industry respect the colorful and consequential past, that doesn't mean that growers, roasters, producers, and others aren't seeking new and exciting tastes and methods. Consider these few examples:

ON THE WEB

>> **Espresso:** Automation is the most exciting innovation in espresso. The focus is on making grinding, dosing, tamping, and extracting more consistent and more easily customized in the hands of an expert barista, which will inevitably enhance the human connection — the barista and customer interaction.

Equally impressive is the work most espresso machine manufacturers are doing to fine-tune the energy efficiency of their equipment. Check out this one example from Arduino at `mailchi.mp`.

Chapters 12 discusses other advances that have been made with espresso machines.

>> **Baristas:** Although crucial to most coffee experiences today, the barista is underpaid and underappreciated. Innovative, forward-thinking coffee businesses are making inroads at improving their lot.

Chapter 12 examines in greater detail barista skill and craftsmanship — the handwork that is involved in creating great espresso coffee.

Climate Change Doesn't Affect Coffee

Coffee is an agricultural product, and it grows across the Coffee Belt — a significant part of the earth in those mountainous areas between the Tropics of Cancer and Capricorn. Part 3 looks more closely at the countries that grow most of the world's coffee crop. Coffee isn't unique. Climate change has affected farmers across the globe, and coffee is no exception.

More specifically, climate plays a significant role throughout the growing, processing, transporting, roasting, and brewing of coffee in the following ways:

>> **Sun:** Coffee plants thrive in dappled sunlight. They do produce when cultivated in open, direct sun, but the life of the tree will be shortened.

>> **Shade:** Shade allows for cover and coffee trees, which need some sun but love some canopy that limits the amount of sun to about two hours each day.

>> **Temperature:** The Coffee Belt is the equatorial belt and coffee loves the temperatures in that climate. Refer to Chapter 5 for more info on ideal temperatures.

>> **Water:** Water is a key element and consistency in amounts and in timing of delivery are essential.

Chapter 5 discusses how weather and climate events or occurrences can impact the smooth seasonal growing and impact the success of the harvest, and in some severe cases, the survival of the trees. If the weather includes abnormal rainfall, increasingly higher temperatures, or intense winds, then farmers, mill owners, shippers, and roasters have to respond.

Elevation is also important. There is a broad temperature range from the bottom of the mountain to the top. Coffee is planted at certain elevations to take advantage of the temperature at that height, and if climate change raises or lowers that temperature, a spot that once was ideal may change enough to make the area less so.

Chapter **16**

Ten (Plus One) Places to Find a Great Cup of Coffee

I n your quest for a great coffee-drinking experience, you may wonder where to go. Although today you can probably find a good, maybe even great, cup of coffee in your local coffeehouse, if you're seeking a great cup of coffee with some extras like historical context or cultural connections then you may have to travel.

My career in coffee has afforded me some incredible opportunities to travel, and during the last 25 years I have enjoyed coffee moments in hundreds of cafés, with thousands of colleagues and friends and one or two curious bystanders who may just have been intrigued by the loudness and passion of my voice. I've had egg coffee in Vietnam, coffee beer in Taiwan, traditional filter coffee in India, siphon brewed in Shanghai, and thousands of simple, delicious Chemex-brewed black coffees. When I travel, coffee is central to my explorations, and in this chapter I share a taste of where you may want to stop for coffee if you're fortunate to be on the road with some free time and brewing curiosity. Of course, this list is nowhere near complete, but these places all have a special place in coffee and in my heart.

San Francisco and the Bay Area

San Francisco and the Bay Area have been central to so much that has brought the coffee industry to where it is today, and because that history is more recent, many of the original people are active and engaged, and their places are still there for you to explore and enjoy.

TIP

A coffee-centered visit to the Bay Area wouldn't be complete without checking out the original **Peets Coffee, Tea & Spices** (www.peets.com) in Berkeley at 2124 Vine Street. Virtually all that's known as specialty coffee for consumers can be linked to Alfred Peet and his vision for something better for them, and this shop was where it all began. You have a good chance of scoring a fine coffee beverage or beautiful roasted beans even today. Chapter 4 discusses Peet's contribution to making a great cup of coffee.

In San Francisco you can find coffee almost everywhere, and each of the known neighborhoods is home to terrific shops. My favorites have always been the locations with links to the heritage of third-wave growth because they've all been significant trendsetters in the development of what is seen globally in coffee shops today:

>> **Caffe Trieste** (http://coffee.caffetrieste.com/)

>> **Equator Coffees** (www.equatorcoffees.com)

>> **Ritual Coffee** (www.ritualroasters.com)

>> **Sightglass Coffee** (www.sightglasscoffee.com)

>> **Verve Coffee** (www.vervecoffee.com)

>> **Wrecking Ball Coffee Roasters** (www.wreckingballcoffee.com)

Whenever I'm in the Bay Area, I always take time to go to Oakland-born, **Blue Bottle Coffee** (www.bluebottlecoffee.com) in the Ferry Building.

Any trip to the Bay Area wouldn't be complete without visiting **Tartine** and exploring some of its **Coffee Manufactory** (www.coffeemanufactory.com/) offerings. Christopher Jordan, another of the unsung heroes of specialty coffee, formerly of Starbucks, Technoserve's East Africa Coffee Initiative, and Verve Coffee Roasters, has joined the Tartine team, who is not only bringing consumers some wonderful coffees and great foods, but also helping guide the coffee industry into the future with its approach to sustainability.

ON THE WEB

Even if a trip to the Bay Area isn't in your plans, you can still access these coffees online.

Portland, Oregon

A trip to Portland, Oregon, is a must, and I'm only a few hours' drive from my Seattle home, so I've made the trip many times.

I suggest you first stop in the Pearl District at **Barista** (www.baristapdx.com). The space is tiny, but the coffee experience is regularly gran; the baristas at Barista are some of the most personable and knowledgeable, and the coffees are always unique and tasty. Barista serves coffees from roasters all over the United States (I was elated to discover a George Howell coffee [refer to Chapter 13] on one visit), and now Barista is roasting coffees as well.

For your second stop on a coffee day tour in Portland is across town at **Coava Roasters** (www.coavacoffee.com), owned by Matt Higgins. Beginning in a garage in North Portland in 2008 and now located in a beautiful shared space with a bamboo furniture showroom, Coava Roasters has a friendly, coffee-centric space where great coffees and a humble, welcoming, and savvy barista team make it all happen.

Well-caffeinated as you may be at this point, the day continues with stops at

- » **Heart Coffee** (www.heartroasters.com)
- » **Sterling Coffee Roasters** (www.sterling.coffee)
- » **Stumptown Coffee Roasters** (www.stumptowncoffee.com) — Portland-born and globally recognized
- » **Water Avenue Coffee Company** (www.wateravenuecoffee.com)

Seattle, Washington

My hometown since 2003, Seattle finishes the West Coast leg of this coffee tour. Not only is Seattle the home of Starbucks, but Seattle also features significantly in the broader history of the birth and growth of specialty coffees. Today Seattle is still home to innovation and almost unrivaled coffee passion.

A visit to Seattle must include a wide array of coffee shops:

- » **Espresso Vivace:** Begin your day at Espresso Vivace (www.espressovivace.com) with an espresso, a macchiato, or a Caffe Nico (a macchiato flavored with orange zest and cinnamon). David Schomer and Geneva Sullivan started Vivace in 1988, and I include a bit more information about Schomer in

Chapter 13. If your visit is in the morning and timed well, you just may encounter him in one of the three locations.

>> **Starbucks Pike Place Market:** Starbucks Pike Place Market store (www. starbucks.com) is something to behold because little has been changed physically since the 1970s when it was built as a dry goods, coffee, tea, and spices merchant. The offerings and experience have changed with the times because today it's all about beverages, whole beans, and souvenirs, all brought to visitors by a talented, multicultural, extraordinarily affable barista team.

>> **La Marzocco's KEXP Café:** Head toward the Space Needle, built for the 1962 World's Fair. Right below it you'll find KEXP Radio. La Marzocco (www.lamarzoc cousa.com), the famed Italian espresso machine manufacturer, has built a museum and café steps away from the DJ booth and the station's reception desk. What makes this spot unique is that each month a different roaster from somewhere in the world is the host, so special coffees and offerings highlight any visit. The host roaster has full control over the menu so you might encounter everything from a traditional Mexican coffee beverage like a *café de olla* (Mexican spiced coffee made with coffee, cinnamon, and raw dark sugar called *piloncillo*) to a lighter roasted, expertly hand-poured Norwegian roaster's best single pour-over.

>> **Milstead Coffee:** A trip to Seattle would be incomplete without a visit to the Fremont neighborhood where Milstead Coffee (http://milsteadandco.com) has been blowing guests away since opening in 2011. Milstead always features an amazing selection of splendid coffees brewed by a superb team of baristas. I discuss founder Andrew Milstead more in Chapter 13.

Seattle isn't suffering from any shortage of good coffee. Here are a few other places you may want to visit:

>> **Analog Coffee** (www.analogcoffee.com)

>> **Elm Coffee Roasters** (www.elmcoffeeroasters.com)

>> **Olympia Coffee Roasters** (www.olympiacoffee.com)

>> **Tougo Coffee** (www.tougocoffee.com)

>> **Victrola Cafe** (www.victrolacoffee.com)

>> **Zoka Coffee Roaster and Tea Company** (www.zokacoffee.com)

I'd be remiss if I didn't guide you to **Starbucks Reserve Roastery** (www.starbucks reserve.com). The first of the six Starbucks Reserve Roasteries in the world (Seattle, Shanghai, Milan, New York City, Tokyo, and Chicago), this striking and lively spot provides visitors with an up-close look at the process of roasting small batches of coffee that I describe in Chapter 10 and couples that experience with a chance to enjoy some innovative coffee and tea beverage creations and some terrific food all served by a consistently expert and personable team.

New York City

New York City is a destination for many things, with coffee no exception. Every block seems to have multiple coffeehouses, lunch counters, sidewalk carts, and groceries that brew coffee, so your choices are abundant. I once read a recent article that counted more than 3,000 coffee shops in the city.

On your next trip to New York City, check out one of these places:

>> **Cafe Grumpy** (www.cafegrumpy.com)

>> **Devoción** (www.devocion.com) and **Toby's Estate Coffee** (www.tobyscoffee.com/): Both of these spots have a familiar, neighborhood ambiance. Located in Williamsburg in Brooklyn, the espresso and drip are great.

>> **Everyman Espresso** (www.everymanespresso.com)

>> **Felix Roasting Co.** (https://felixroastingco.com)

>> **Sey Coffee** (www.seycoffee.com)

New York also has plenty of West Coast coffeehouses. You can try Portland's Stumptown at the Ace Hotel, Oakland's Blue Bottle, and Seattle's Starbucks Reserve Roastery.

Vienna, Austria

Since 1683, when the first coffeehouse opened in Vienna (refer to Chapter 3), the city has maintained a unique coffee culture that celebrates that heritage and brings a formality and food to a café visit that is quite special.

You can find the standard global brands like Starbucks and Austrian chains Aida and Oberlaa in Vienna, but if you want to make your visit truly memorable, then focus on my list of noteworthy spots. Be prepared for experiences that involve formally dressed waiters, table service, and somewhat unfamiliar drink names, such as

>> **Mélange:** My favorite. A wonderful beverage made of espresso, a splash of hot water, and a healthy layer of fresh steamed milk

>> **Grosser Schwarzer:** A double espresso

>> **Einspänner:** Known to be a favorite for the horse carriage drivers because it's a glass of espresso topped with a generous glob of whipped cream that keeps the sloshing and cooling to a minimum

The coffeehouse experience is incomplete without an accompaniment of extraordinary Viennese pastries. The choices are overwhelming.

Here is my list of great spots for you to try:

>> **Café Central:** Visit to admire the architectural splendor of Café Central (`www.cafecentral.wien/en/`) and then feast on an extensive array of coffees, pastries, and heartier fare.

>> **Café Hawelka:** A family-run enterprise since 1939, Café Hawelka (`https://hawelka.at`) is popular with artists and politicians. Its signature dish, the Buchtein, a custard accompanied brioche pastry, is great with any one of their diverse coffee offerings.

>> **Café Landtmann:** Open since 1873, this intimate Viennese café (`www.landtmann.at`) with its dark wood is known for its exquisite coffees and exceptionally beautiful pastries all served by a traditionally dressed, but congenial staff.

>> **Kaffee Alt Wien:** This café (`www.kaffeealtwien.at`) is younger, dating to 1922, and features a wonderful range of coffees.

Rome, Italy

Italy features significantly in coffee history (refer to Chapters 3 and 4), and Rome makes my list as a top place to visit for a coffee tour because it so admirably represents a country that is passionate about its coffee, coffeehouses, and heritage. "*Un caffè per favore*" (A coffee, please) will get you an espresso at hundreds of fast-paced, stand-up coffee bars, and you'll enjoy joining the majority of coffee drinkers by repeating that experience a few times during an average day.

You can find an incredible cup of coffee at these places:

>> **Sant' Eustachio Il Caffè:** The 1930s introduced espresso (see Chapter 12). That same decade also saw the opening of this place. This café (`https://santeustachioilcaffe.com/en/`) is immensely popular, and many locals visit to enjoy its signature *zuccherato,* which is a sweetened espresso executed by adept barista craftsmanship that mixes the sugar and the first few drops of espresso and creates a kind of whipped foamy consistency.

>> **Antigua Tazza del Oro:** Another café of note not only for its awesome espresso beverage menu, but also for a splendid Italian *granita,* a slushy ice drink that hits the spot on a warm Italian day in Antigua Tazza del Oro (`www.tazzadorocoffeeshop.com`).

>> **Sciascia Caffè 1919:** This century-old and lovely café (`https://sciascia caffe1919.it`) is quaint, and be sure to look for its signature beverage that incorporates sweet, espresso-melted dark chocolate on the sides of the demi-tasse cup.

>> **Faro–Luminaries of Coffee** (`www.farorome.com`) and **Tram Depot:** These two newer cafés in this tradition-laden coffee scene have gained notoriety, because they both bridge the old with the new wave. These coffee shops have brought some of the third-wave coffee breadth and a more international feel to the staid Italian coffee culture and are worth a look.

Oslo, Norway

Once each month for the past few months I've received a small bit of Oslo's robust coffee world in my mailbox in Seattle in the form of a small bag of fresh roasted coffee from **Tim Wendelboe's** (`https://timwendelboe.no`), which I strongly recommend. A visit would no doubt reinforce the generous presence he has established in the coffee community as a teacher and innovative pioneer.

Norway is ranked second in the world for per capita coffee consumption (behind Finland) with an average annual consumption of almost 10 kg. Hence, Oslo has no shortage of coffeehouses, and here are my top recommendations. They all feature top-notch barista teams who can create a memorable cup of coffee:

>> **Erlik Kaffe** (`www.erlikkaffe.no`)

>> **Fuglen** (`www.fuglen.no`)

>> **Hendrix Ibsen** (`http://hendrixibsen.rocks`)

>> **Mocca** (`www.facebook.com/moccaoslo/`)

>> **Stockfleths** (`https://stockfleths.as`)

>> **Supreme Roastworks** (`www.srw.no`)

Reykjavik, Iceland

Even before you leave the Keflavik Airport in Reykjavik, you don't have to look far. **Kaffitár** (`https://kaffitar.is`), one of Iceland's most well-known and innovative coffee sources, has a shop right inside the airport. Kaffitár has been around since 1990, and owners Aðalheiður Héðinsdottir and husband Eiríkur Hilmarrson have done a noble job at directly nurturing relationships with multiple coffee farms, enabling them to bring customers on a high-quality, virtual world tour at every visit. They have multiple shops in Reykjavik, so make sure you visit one when you're in Iceland.

Coffee is second on my list of priorities when visiting any city with historic museums, and Reykjavik allows me to entertain my love of both by visiting the Reykjavik Art Museum and **Iða Zimsen,** which is right next door. Iða Zimsen is a bookstore and a café, and the pleasant ambience affords a chance to relax with a great coffee and a wide range of things to read.

Here are some suggestions to seek an incredible cup of coffee:

>> **Bismút** (www.facebook.com/bismutreykjavik/)

>> **Café Babalú** (www.facebook.com/Cafe-Babalú)

>> **Floran Garden Bistro** (www.floran.is/floranenglish)

>> **Kaffihus Vesturbæjar** (www.kaffihusvesturbaejar.is)

>> **Reykjavik Roasters** (https://reykjavikroasters.is/en/)

>> **Stofan Café**

>> **Te og Kaffi** (www.teogkaffi.is)

>> **Vinyl** (https://kaffi-vinyl.business.site)

Mokka Kaffi (www.mokka.is), which opened in 1958, is older than many on this list and was the first to have an espresso machine and offer coffees inspired by traditional Italian coffee bars. Not only does it accomplish more than a chance to enjoy some good coffee, but it also offers a look back across more than 60 years of Reykjavik's coffee culture.

Taipei, Taiwan

Taipei may not be your final destination, but you can still enjoy a great cup of coffee here. A vibrant, immaculate, and welcoming metropolis, Taipei guarantees some opportunities to explore and experiment with coffee. Past world coffee champions hailing from Taiwan include Berg Wu (Barista, 2016), Chad Wang (Brewers Cup, 2017), Pang-Yu Liu (World Cup Tasters, 2014), and Jacky Lai (Roasting, 2014).

Here are my suggestions:

» **Fika-Fika:** A wide range of beautiful single-origin coffees greet you as you arrive at Fika-Fika (www.fikafikacafe.com), and the barista team is quite adept whether you order brewed or an espresso coffee. This is a lively meeting place for local coffee aficionados.

» **Maven Coworking Café:** This café (www.mavencoffee.co) is a wonderful coworking space. Located in the Zhongshan District, this shop always features a variety of beautiful coffees prepared by some of the most personable, talented baristas to be found anywhere. Ask for a tasty treat to accompany your coffee.

» **Simple Kaffa:** Berg Wu, 2016 World Barista Champion, co-owns this charming café (https://simplekaffa.com/) in a downstairs area at the Hotel V. You can enjoy beautifully crafted, pour-over coffees and some tasty pastry tidbits for pairings.

» **Starbucks:** You may be surprised at me suggesting you stop at Starbucks (www.starbucks.com.tw/), Taipei 101 B1 Reserve Bar, located at B1F, No. 45 Shifu Road, Xinyi Dist. in the Taipei 101 building. You won't be disappointed by this café at any time of the day actually because of its striking design and the stellar barista team. Start with an americano, double short, a great early day Starbucks beverage, and my favorite when I visit there.

» **VWI by Chad Wang:** This café (https://beanshipper.com/collections/vwi-by-chadwang) is two-story but small and easy to miss from the street. Inside it's elegant and beautifully decorated and leaves no doubt that coffee is the focus. Order any one of the many coffees, as a hand-pour given the owner is a world champion brewer.

Melbourne, Australia

Down Under also has a plethora of places you can visit to find that perfect cup of coffee. Melbourne, Australia's second largest city, has plenty of options that are representative of the combined high-quality and well-crafted experiences that are possible in the hundreds of cafés in Melbourne. A few suggestions include

» **Aunty Peg's** (www.proudmarycoffee.com.au/pages/aunty-pegs-1)

» **Axil Coffee Roasters** (https://axilcoffee.com.au): Owned by David Makin, three-time national barista title winner

» **Dukes** (www.dukescoffee.com.au)

» **Industry Beans** (https://industrybeans.com)

- >> **Market Lane Coffee** (https://marketlane.com.au)

- >> **Proud Mary Coffee Roasters** (www.proudmarycoffee.com.au)

- >> **Rumble Coffee Roasters** (www.rumblecoffee.com.au)

- >> **St Ali** (https://stali.com.au)

- >> **Seven Seeds** (https://sevenseeds.com.au)

- >> **Wide Open Road** (https://wideopenroad.com.au)

Short black (espresso), long black (americano), latte, or flat white are smart orders for your first order because the Melbourne cafés will offer consistent but varied experiences with each. You can compare and contrast with the wide variety.

With Melbourne, perhaps more than in any other city in this chapter, appreciate the focus on special coffee roasts, multiple dairy selections, and a passion for amazing results in the cup that is heralded and pretty much unrivaled.

Addis Ababa, Ethiopia

Although you may not be heading to Ethiopia soon or ever, this is where coffee started (see Chapter 3), so if you're a true coffee afficionado, you may want to consider a trip there. Although I've never been to Ethiopia, I've heard these coffeeshops are must-visits in Addis Adaba:

- >> **Café Choche** (www.facebook.com/CafeChoche)

- >> **Harar Coffee** also known as **Mokarar** (www.facebook.com/mokarar.coffee/)

- >> **Kaldi's Coffee** (http://kaldiscoffeeethiopia.com)

- >> **Lime Tree** (www.facebook.com/LimeTreeAddis/)

- >> **Tomoca** (www.tomocacoffee.com) is one of the oldest coffee spots in Addis Adaba. A short walk in the vicinity presents more coffee stalls in bars and restaurants.

- >> **Yeshi Buna** (https://yeshi-buna-ethio-african-cafe-and.business.site)

You may never have the opportunity to go to Ethiopia to enjoy the coffee, so you can experience Ethiopia here. I've fortunately been a guest at a few traditional Ethiopian coffee ceremonies, *jebena buna* in the local Amharic language, so seek one out if you can. These types of events celebrate coffee and the long-standing, robust coffee culture.

A ceremony, often hosted by a young woman of the house, begins with roasting and savoring the intense aromatics of roasted coffee and sometimes incense, flowers, and grasses. Brewing follows, and it involves using a *jebana*, the brewing apparatus in which water is boiled and eventually the coffee ground is added. After it's brewed, the coffee is served in small cups called *finjals*. This process is repeated with new water added to the grounds in the jebana and boiled. Although the coffee is a bit weaker, the connection and warmth of community intensifies.

The three rounds are

» *Abol* or *awel*

» *Tona*

» *Bereka*

Each carries spiritual meaning with the bereka, representing a blessing and a wonderful sendoff.

Japan

Thousands of coffee spots in every major city in Japan bear witness to the popularity of coffee. Perhaps nowhere is the coffee and service culture as lively or long-standing as Tokyo, Kyoto, Osaka, and Fukuoka. I've been surprised and delighted during my visits to those cities. In fact, I've enjoyed some of the most memorable coffee experiences and developed treasured friendships there.

REMEMBER

Not many coffee afficionados are aware of the high-end coffee experiences in Japan through a *kissaten*. Dating back to the 1920s, a kissaten is a tea shop that serves coffee and also serves sweets or food.

Here are some kissaten I recommend:

» **Café Bach:** My visit to Café Bach (www.bach-kaffee.co.jp/) started with a 20-minute wait outside on a cold February day with a group of friends. When we were invited into the small space, I was struck by the aroma of coffee and the warmth. A long counter with pour-over gear stood in front of an array of containers holding roasted beans and a roasting machine. The selection included 14 or 15 coffees, and I enjoyed both a Guatemala Antigua and an Ethiopia Natural, both made by our barista at the brew bar.

» **Chatei Hatou:** Only a short few hundred yards from the famed Shibuya crossing, this kissaten has withstood the test and competition of the global and small Japanese coffee shops. It still incorporates an older pour-over coffee style; your brewer may take as long as 20 minutes to craft your delicious cup. That brewer will finish by selecting a cup and saucer for you that may be color coordinated to what you're wearing.

In contrast to the look back that current kissaten provide, every major Japanese city also has a vibrant café scene where you can find an incredible array of tiny spots for coffee in virtually every neighborhood. Often staffed by the owner or owners, each offers a unique expression of those owners' vision of coffee, community, attention to detail, and craft.

Here are a few notable cafés:

>> **Aeru** (https://aerucoffeestop.stores.jp/)

>> **All Seasons Coffee,** also known as 4/4 Seasons Coffee (https://allseasons coffee.jp/)

>> **Cobi Coffee** (http://bloom-branch.jp/news/cobicoffee-news)

>> **Passage Coffee** (https://passagecoffee.com)

A trip to Japan wouldn't be complete without a visit to these two multinational coffee forces that have found inspiration and established a following in Tokyo:

>> **Kiyosumi Shirakawa Roastery & Café:** Blue Bottle coffee's founder, James Freeman, has spoken often of his being inspired by the Japanese coffee experience in creating Oakland-based Blue Bottle, and you can find a few Blue Bottle shops in Tokyo. I suggest this café, which opened in 2015. I waited more than two hours just a few weeks after it opened and enjoyed some lovely hand-poured coffees and strikingly beautiful and tasty pastries.

>> **Starbucks Reserve Tokyo Roastery:** Although Starbucks coffee has thousands of stores throughout Japan, none is more striking and worthy of a visit than the Starbucks Reserve Tokyo Roastery (www.starbucksreserve.com/en-us/locations/tokyo). Located in the hip Meguro neighborhood, this four-story spot is architecturally stunning. It offers unique, roasted in-house coffees, a wide array of creative coffee and tea beverages, and some stellar and varied foods. I highly recommend making an effort to connect directly with your barista, server, or one of the team roasters and give them an opportunity to share some of their passion and craft. The team at this roastery is one of the best in the world at bringing to life great service and finely tuned coffee craftsmanship.

Appendixes

Appendix **A**

Glossary

AA: Size designation of green coffee considered top offering and most often seen from Kenya. There are multiple size grades, including E, PB, AB, C, TT, T, and MH/ML.

acidity: Bright, tart mouthfeel description used in coffee tasting. Acidity (along with flavor, aroma, and body) is one of the principal categories used by professional tasters in cupping or individuals sensorily evaluating coffee.

AeroPress: A brewing device incorporating immersion and pressure.

affogato: An Italian dessert made with espresso or strong black coffee covering ice cream.

after-dinner roast: A dark roast similar to French roast and Italian roast.

aftertaste: The finish or residual flavors remaining after tasting.

aged coffee: Historically, coffee's taste characteristics that were impacted by being held in the holds of ships for a lengthy period while in transit. Today some coffee companies deliberately orchestrate the process to develop a woody, musty flavor profile in the coffee when roasted and tasted.

American roast: Medium roast coffee thought to be most preferred by traditional American coffee drinkers.

americano: Espresso beverage tracing its history to the U.S. troops stationed in Italy in World War II. Espresso shots diluted with hot water.

Arabian mocha: Coffee blend comprised of Arabian coffees from Yemen and the Port of Mokha. Considered the first blend.

Arabica: The earliest cultivated species of coffee tree and still the most widely grown. Arabica crops comprise approximately 70 percent of the world's coffee. *See also* **Coffea Canephora** and **Robusta**.

aroma: The smell of the coffee. Along with flavor, acidity, and body, aroma is one of the principal categories used by professional tasters in cupping or individuals sensorily evaluating coffee.

ashy: Flavor also referred to as roasty and devoid of complex characteristics.

aspiration: Also called *slurping,* this action gets the coffee into the mouth with air and virtually sprays it across the palate. *Cuppers,* the term used to describe professional coffee tasters, find this allows them to attain a more pronounced sensory evaluation.

astringent: Describes drying mouthfeel.

baggy: Aroma or taste that is reminiscent of paper bag. Often associated with green coffee that has been stored too long before roasting.

baked: Roast quality absent of complexity and nuance. Often caused by spending too much time in the drying stage of the roasting process.

balance: Evenness across complexities that are present, but no one element overwhelms the others.

barista: Italian for a skilled, experienced coffee professional.

batch roaster: Roasting machine in which distinct batches are completed.

bird friendly: Coffee grown in environments where birds flourish and their habitat is maintained.

biscotti: Italian hard cookie, often served with coffee.

bitter: One characteristic of overextracted brews as well as overroasted coffees and those with various taste defects; caffeine contributes some bitterness to all coffee. Bitter is sometimes a harsh, unpleasant taste. Dark roasts are intentionally bitter.

blade grinder: A small kitchen grinder with a chamber in which a spinning blade chops the coffee.

blend: Two or more coffees combined.

Blue Mountain: Famed Jamaican growing region.

body: The sensation of heaviness, richness, or thickness, or even thinness and lightness, and associated texture when tasting coffee. Body, along with flavor, acidity, and aroma, is one of the principal categories used by professional tasters cupping or individuals sensorily evaluating coffee. Body also defines one of the three parts of an espresso shot. *See also* **crema, heart, espresso.**

boiler: Internal espresso machine part where water in heated and stored.

bouquet: Fragrance, aroma, nose, and aftertaste combined.

breve: Latte in which half and half is used for the dairy component.

brewing: Any method where water and coffee are brought together to produce a beverage.

bright: *See also* **acidity.**

briny: Saltiness. Often experienced with coffee sitting on a warm burner for an extended time period.

burr: A revolving abrasive surface in a grinder. Two burrs are precisely spaced to ensure that roasted coffee beans grinding between them are uniformly ground.

burr grinder: Coffee grinder with two discs or burrs that can be adjusted for particle size adjustment.

C.A.F.E Practices: Coffee and Farmer Equity Practices are Starbucks' comprehensive green coffee–sourcing guidelines, developed in collaboration with Conservation International, that take a comprehensive approach to ethically sourcing green coffee globally by evaluating economic, social, and environmental aspects of coffee production.

cafe au lait: Brewed coffee with warmed or steamed milk added.

caffeine: The drug contained in coffee and tea. It's what makes coffee so addictive. It stimulates the central nervous system and in the right amounts causes adrenaline to be released.

cappuccino: Espresso beverage comprised of espresso, steamed milk, and a thin layer of distinct foam.

CBB damage: Coffee cherry that has been eaten by the borer beetle.

chaff: By-product created when roasted coffee expands. Almost like sawdust or peanut skin, it's removed in the final stages of roasting.

Chiapas: Mexican state known for outstanding coffee.

chicory: A somewhat woody, perennial herbaceous plant sometimes added to ground coffee as an additive to stretch the quantity.

chocolatey: The taste or aroma of chocolate. Some coffees (Central American and Yemeni) have a distinct chocolatey aroma and even feature a slightly bittersweet chocolate taste on occasion.

cinnamon roast: A light to medium roast whose name derives from the color of cinnamon.

citrus: Often seen in coffee and used to define both the aromatic and taste qualities often reminiscent of ripe citrus fruit.

city roast: A medium roast.

clean: Flavorful but without any unusual, edgy, or pungent attributes.

Coffea Canephora: Commonly known as *Robusta,* it's the second most cultivated type of coffee. *See also* **Arabica.**

coffee berry borer: Insect that bores through the cherry and ruins it.

coffee cherry: Fruit of the coffee tree. Each cherry contains two regular coffee beans (really the seeds) or one peaberry.

coffee future: Commodities transaction based not on present, but rather a future market price.

coffee leaf rust: A airborne fungus that forms on a coffee tree leaf and prevents any photosynthesis from occurring, thereby destroying any potential yield.

cold brew: Sweet, low-acidity coffee beverage created/brewed using a brewing method in which cold water and an extended coffee grounds and water contact time achieve extraction.

complexity: Taste seemingly multilayered, giving the impression of fullness and vibrancy. Blends of coffees are often created with complexity as a goal though individual coffees can present complexity.

cowboy coffee: Also known as *campfire coffee,* this coffee is brewed by boiling coarse grounds in a simple pot. After being heated and then removed from the heat, the grounds settle in the pot and the coffee is poured.

crema: The lighter brown or tan top layer of an espresso shot. Formed by miniscule air bubbles and emulsified coffee oils.

crust: A layer of coffee grounds that form at the top when cupping. The action of *breaking the crust* is a key step in the cupping process that both allows for an assessment of the aroma and also serves to move the coffee around and impact the brewing extraction.

cuppers: Professional coffee tasters.

cupping: Tasting procedure used by coffee professionals. Coffee grounds and hot water are combined in a shallow bowl with subsequent slurping from spoons dipped in the upper 2/3 of the cup.

dark roast: Dark brown roast, sometimes from oily beans.

decaffeinated: Coffee that has the caffeine nearly eliminated prior to roasting and brewing.

dehulled: The process of removing the outer layers of the coffee cherry to get to the bean.

doppio: Italian espresso beverage with two shots of espresso.

dose: The amount of coffee used.

doser: A spring-loaded device on specialized espresso grinders that dispenses single servings of ground coffee.

doser grinder: A specialized espresso grinder that has a feature that allows it to deliver predetermined amounts of precisely measured coffee doses.

double: Two espresso shots.

drip coffee: Brewed coffee made from water heated in the coffee maker and dripped through ground coffee in a filter basket directly into the cup or pot. Filter-drip coffee makers are the most popular type of home coffee brewers used today.

drip tray: The deck on an espresso machine beneath the brew head where the barista places the cup or shot glasses.

dry: A taste description term for astringent.

dry process: A method for removing the husk or fruit after the coffee fruit has been dried.

earthy: Coffee with the taste of fresh earth, wet soil, or raw potatoes. Although sometimes a negative characteristic, in some Indonesian semi-dry (semi-washed) coffees, it defines a most cherished attribute.

elephant beans: A descriptor for extra-large coffee beans; also known as *Maragogipe,* named after a city in Brazil. A variety of Arabica coffee.

espresso: Approximately an ounce (single) or 2-ounce (double) beverage created by a high pressure extraction at approximately 9 bar pressure from approximately 8 (single) or 15 grams (double) of fine, evenly ground coffee, evenly distributed, and compacted into what's known as a *puck.*

espresso con panna: Beverage where one or two shots of espresso is topped with whipped cream.

espresso machine: An espresso machine forces hot water at 9 to 10 bars of pressure through very finely ground coffee beans. The machine also features a steaming mechanism to aerate and heat milk.

espresso pod: Pre-measured coffee dose in small capsule designed to be inserted in an automatic espresso machine for precise extraction.

estate: A coffee farm or plantation.

Fair Trade: A private program that certifies farmers are receiving a fair minimum price for their coffee crop.

fermentation: The microbial reaction of yeasts and bacteria breaking down the sugars in mucilage. This process produces acids that will later add complexity and depth to a coffee. The most common method that allows for fermentation is *wet processing.*

filter basket: The basket that coffee is placed in to allow for filter brewing. The basket may have holes or be lined with paper.

first crack: Also known as *first pop,* the first of two distinctly different periods of cracking sounds during a roast, when the coffee beans are giving off their own heat and expanding suddenly. Begins around 400°F and sounds like popcorn.

flat: Coffee that is without aroma and flavor.

flat white: An espresso beverage like a latte but traditionally and passionately more defined by a singular size, 6 ounces with two shots of espresso.

flavored coffee: Roasted coffee that has been sprayed with flavoring. Often the least expensive coffees used as the flavorings are quite strong and overcome any nuances that may have been present in the unflavored bean.

floaters: Coffee cherries that float in water and are removed in the early stages of washed processing. They float because they're overripe, damaged, or deformed.

floral: The scent of flowers sometimes perceived in coffees. These scents can be quite wide ranging.

French press: A brewer invented in the mid-1800s. This classic immersion apparatus is also called a *plunger pot*. It's comprised of a vessel to hold the coffee and hot water and a plunger assembly that holds a screen that serves as a filter when plunged.

French roast: A roast level description often at the darkest point in the roast spectrum. Although certainly a favorite of many coffee drinkers for its smoky, low acidity, limited body flavor characteristics, coffee drinkers who treasure sweetness, crisp acidity, and complexity also criticize it for its absence of those characteristics.

freshness: Like any fresh fruit or vegetable, this characteristic is essential to good coffee flavor. Green, unroasted coffee can maintain a level of freshness for a year or two; roasted whole beans protected from oxygen, light, heat, and moisture can up to six to eight months. After exposed, the clock is ticking and the beans will fade dramatically over a two- to three-week period. Ground coffee loses its freshness even faster.

frothing: The steaming process accomplished with a steam wand of an espresso machine to create carefully aerated, velvety foam used in many espresso beverages.

fruity: The aroma or taste of fruit that many coffees exhibit.

gicleur: A small opening used in espresso machine group heads to limit the flow of water. Italian but derived from the French verb *gicler,* which means "to squirt."

gourmet coffee: Specialty or premium coffee; also used to define the descriptor of high-grown, Arabica coffees that are noteworthy for their unique flavor profile highlighted by potential sweetness, complexity, and a remarkable range of acidity, body, and flavor.

grande: Italian for large, a 16-ounce beverage. Starbucks is responsible for widespread use of this size descriptor.

grassy: An aroma linked to fresh mowed grass, green foliage, herbs, or unripe fruit. Often associated with sour-tasting underroasted coffees or water-damaged, poorly dried green coffees.

green coffee: Unroasted but processed coffee beans. Also a negative descriptor for underroasted brewed coffee.

grind/grounds: The small particles created by grinding whole roasted beans. The brewing method dictates the grind size, and the extraction from the grind into the brewing hot water is dependent on many factors with grind particle size being one of the most important.

Grounds for Health (GFH): A Mexican and Central American international nonprofit created to provide healthcare services to coffee communities.

group/group head: The connecting point on an espresso machine where the portafilter is inserted. It's where the heated water meets the dosed coffee contained in the portafilter.

half caf: A coffee drink descriptor for a beverage made with half regular coffee and half decaffeinated coffee. Sometimes called a *split shot*.

hard bean: Refers to the growing altitude and a link that exists between the slower maturation of the cherry that occurs as you move up the mountain. Hard bean (HB) and Strictly hard bean (SHB), grown above 4,500 feet above sea level, attribute their consistency and often fine taste qualities to that slower maturation.

harmless: Nonfat, decaffeinated coffee beverage.

harvesting: Process of identifying and collecting coffee cherry at the peak of ripeness. With higher grown Arabica, the beans are picked by hand in often mountainous, difficult, steep terrain.

heart: The bottom layer of an espresso shot. *See also* **crema** and **body.**

herbal: Tasting descriptor inspired by herbs.

hidey: Noting the smell or taste of leather.

hulling: The process of removing the parchment layer or hull that surrounds the coffee bean in the coffee cherry.

iced latte: Iced version of this espresso and milk beverage. *See also* **latte.**

iced mocha: Iced version of this espresso, chocolate, and milk beverage. *See also* **mocha latte.**

ICO: *See also* **International Coffee Organization.**

India monsoon: Aged Indian coffee distinguished by a golden color (unroasted bean) and a mellow taste. Exposure to the elements in monsoon conditions impacts coffees being transported by ship over many month journeys.

The International Coffee Organization (ICO): An intergovernmental organization that fosters collaboration to accomplish problem-solving in the global coffee industry and promotes improved standards in developing countries.

Irish coffee: Beverage made with brewed coffee, Irish Whiskey, sugar, and finished with aerated heavy cream.

Italian roast: A dark roast featuring a dark brown color and oily bean surface.

KVW: *See also* **Kaffee Veredelungs Werk.**

Kaffee Veredelungs Werk (KVW): A German company that decaffeinates coffees using the methylene chloride method (MC), one of the most popular methods used to decaffeinate. The U.S. Food and Drug Administration has established it safe because the chemical is destroyed by boiling and heat from roasting.

knock box: The box, pan, or drawer adjacent to an espresso machine used for disposal of spent grounds from the portafilter. The barista knocks the portafilter to force the grounds to drop out.

kopi luwak: Coffee from Sumatra, Indonesia, noteworthy by the unique way it's processed — the seed (the bean) and the fruit are separated. A mammal called a luwak, or civet, eats ripe coffee cherries, digests the fruit, and excretes the seeds, after which the seeds or beans are gathered from its dry droppings. It's one of the most expensive coffees in the world because it's so rare. Akin to an average Latin or Central American washed coffee with medium acidity and body and simple flavors.

latte: A shot or two of espresso combined with freshly aerated, steamed milk. *Caffé latte* is coffee with milk in Italian.

latte art: A barista-executed, creative design on the surface of a variety of milk and espresso beverages. Executed by hand-pouring milk through the espresso or pouring and then using toothpicks or a variety of tools, syrups, or sprinkles to give an espresso drink the perfect finishing touch.

macchiato: Italian meaning "spotted" — can be espresso macchiato as well as latte macchiato. The espresso version features a shot or two of espresso with a spoonful of freshly steamed, aerated milk. The latte version is freshly aerated steamed milk through which a shot or two of espresso is poured, leaving a brown dot on an otherwise white surface.

malty: Inspired by the smell of malt. Cereal and toast-like are often associated.

medicinal: The aroma of medicine, sometimes specific to iodine. This attribute can occur if cherry is left to dry on coffee tree.

medium roast: Medium brown-colored coffee.

methylene chloride: Chemical used in decaffeination process. *See also* **Kaffee Veredelungs Werk.**

mocha java: *See also* **Arabian mocha.**

mocha latte: Latte incorporating chocolate as an ingredient.

moka pot: A stovetop espresso maker that incorporates pressure in the brew cycle.

monsooned: Descriptor for modern aging and exposure process thought to replicate more extended exposure that occurred on shipping vessels hundreds of years ago.

mottled: Descriptor for unroasted green coffee with significant discoloration and unevenness of color. Thought to be brought on by uneven drying.

mucilage: The sticky layer of a coffee cherry between the outer skin and the seed/bean.

musty: A taste or aroma of mold. Sometimes resulting when coffee is stored damp or dried too slowly. Often-negative attribute description also positively assesses monsoon coffee and aged coffee.

nel drip: Abbreviated from the flannel from which this drip brewing device is made, the nel drip gained original popularity hundreds of years ago in Japan. Achieving good consistent results is difficult because the flannel filter, or cloth sock, is tough to keep pristine; the best method dictates that it's stored in a refrigerator.

new crop: Recently harvested or current crop.

nose: The aroma and taste attributed from a coffee breathed by the nose.

nutty: The aroma and taste attributes of fresh nuts.

oniony: Flavor sensations of onions. Sometimes caused by stagnant water during washed coffee processing.

organic: Certification associated with no pesticide use and strict soil management.

outer skin: The thickest and outermost top layer of the coffee cherry.

overextracted: When too much of the soluble flavors are taken from a coffee dose. Describes results with bitter, dry, astringent qualities.

papery: A taste reminiscent of paper sometimes attributed to whole beans being stored in paper; sometimes in brewing the coffee drips through low quality or unrinsed paper filters.

parchment: The internal layer of a coffee cherry that surrounds the bean.

parchment coffee: Unroasted coffee with the skin and pulp removed.

past crop: Green coffee that has been stored. *See also* **new crop.**

peaberry: Unlike the usual two, flat-sided beans, peaberry beans have formed as one in the cherry. A peaberry occurs 3 to 5 percent of the time and is often simply left mixed among the more ordinary beans. Sometimes peaberries are separated out and often bring higher prices. Although it's questionable that peaberries taste different from normal beans, the intense extra work that is involved in sorting them makes them unique.

percolator: A brewing method popular until the early 1970s; it recycles boiling or almost boiling water and eventually the actual coffee over the grounds continuously throughout the brew cycle. The combination of higher temperature and recirculating brewed coffee often results in overextracted results.

piston espresso machine: Espresso machine in which the water pressure needed is achieved by a manual piston device and a barista-operated lever.

portafilter: A handled device that contains a filter basket that holds espresso and clamps onto the group head. A bottomless or naked portafilter is one that has no pour spouts, exposing the bottom of the espresso basket.

puck: The tamped, compressed coffee dose inside the portafilter used for espresso extraction. When knocked out of the portafilter into the knock box, it sometimes remains whole and resembles a small hockey puck.

pulled long: Also called *espresso lungo;* an espresso shot that has been extracted longer than the normal 20 to 30 seconds and finishes with increased volume; has more caffeine and tastes bitterer.

pulled short: Also called *espresso ristretto,* which is Italian for "espresso shrunk" or "made narrow." An espresso shot that has been extracted less that the normal 20 to 30 seconds yielding less volume and more concentrated, less bitter attributes.

pulp: The layer of mucilage between the skin and pit of the coffee cherry. With a texture like a grape, its sweetness varies depending on the level of ripeness and developed sugars. The layer is often thin, so although it's sometimes tasty, there is little of it.

pulping: Removing the outer layers of the coffee cherry.

quad: An espresso drink with four shots.

red eye: Also called a *shot in the dark* or *eye opener,* this beverage is brewed coffee to which a shot or two of espresso has been added.

Robusta: Also referred to as *Coffee Canephora,* it's the second most abundantly harvested coffee (behind Arabica). Robusta coffee trees can be grown at lower elevations; they also have better disease and insect tolerance and larger yields. Robusta would seem to be a better option for global coffee farmers were it not for its rather harsh, often unpleasant flavor attributes.

rubbery: The aroma and flavor characteristics of tires or rubber bands.

SCAA: *See also* **Specialty Coffee Association of America.**

second crack: Also known as *second pop,* it refers to the later stage of the roasting process when the heat in the roaster rises to 440 to 450°F, actively cooking coffee beans.

semidry process: Also known as *semi-washed,* refers to coffees that have the skin removed, go into brief storage, get a washing usually by hand, and are dried. After some drying, the coffee beans are dehulled, sorted, and placed in bags for shipping. This process is common in the Indonesian islands of Sulawesi and Sumatra and sometimes in Brazil.

shot: An espresso serving. Shot volume size is usually one ounce for a single, two for a double.

silver skin: A very thin membrane or layer that remains on coffee beans after the hull is removed. It can be polished off but generally remains until the roasting stage, where it's removed as *chaff.*

single origin: Coffee from a single country, growing region, or farm.

siphon: A complicated brewing device that utilizes vacuum pressure and multiple containers during the brewing cycle where water and then coffee pass back and forth because of pressure variations. It's celebrated for its theatrical presentation and for producing flavorful but thin coffee.

skinny: An espresso beverage made with nonfat dairy.

slow-dripper: Often remarkably intricate glass tubing and containers highlight this brewing device. Coffee and water together drip slowly through grounds and tubes. Twelve hours later is a vessel of cold brew-like coffee.

slurping: *See also* **aspiration.**

smooth: A balanced coffee with no discernable flavors or aftertastes. Sometimes called *round* or *soft.*

solo: A single shot or an espresso beverage with one shot.

sorting: A process where green coffee beans are sorted by hand to remove defects.

sour: A dominant, biting, sharp, and unpleasant flavor attribute. Vinegar or acetic acid tastes sour. Often confused with *acidity,* which is a brighter, livelier attribute.

Specialty Coffee Association of America (SCAA): The global organization that sets the standards for growing, roasting, and brewing and celebrates a membership comprised of people from all parts of the coffee industry.

spicey: Aromatic and flavor descriptor associated with sweet spices like cloves, cinnamon, or allspice.

steam wand: A stem on an espresso machine that allows the barista to control steam flow and create creamy, aerated milk.

steaming pitcher: Specialized, stainless steel container used by the barista when engaging the steam wand to create creamy, aerated milk.

Swiss water process: A 100 percent chemical-free coffee decaffeination process.

tall: A 12-ounce coffee beverage size popularized by Starbucks.

tamper: A device used to compress a measured dose of coffee in the portafilter basket.

tamping: The action of compressing ground espresso needed to compact the coffee evenly to avoid channeling. About 30 pounds of pressure is ideal.

thin: Descriptive term for coffee that is watery, weak, and with little or no body.

Turkish coffee: A coffee beverage created by combining extremely fine ground coffee with hot water.

Utz: Formerly referred to as *Utz Certified,* this program is a detailed set of social and environmental criteria for responsible growing practices and efficient farm management.

valve bag: An airtight bag with a small one-way valve that allows for elements to pass from inside to outside but doesn't allow the reverse. As fresh roasted coffee gives off quite a lot of carbon dioxide gas, the valve allows for the gas to escape but doesn't allow air, the enemy of freshness, to get in.

varietal: Coffee derived from a single cultivar; sometimes more universally used to describe a coffee from a single region or country.

venti: A 20-ounce coffee beverage popularized by Starbucks.

Vienna roast: A roast level that is often the lightest of the darker roasts. Also known as *full city* or *full flavor*, this roast level can deliver great flavor and aroma, despite being a bit darker.

wet: A variation of an espresso beverage where more milk and less foam are used. *Dry* is the reverse — less liquid and more foam.

wet mill: Facility for processing coffee cherry using the wet or washed process.

wet process: A method for removing the husk or fruit after the coffee cherry fruit has been picked. Water is used to help facilitate that removal.

Appendix B

Timeline of Key History of Coffee

Coffee has played a part in world history for a long time. Knowing some of the key milestones has helped me understand how significant moments long ago impact what has become the modern world of coffee. Here are some important dates to remember:

200 B.C.: Coffee is cultivated in Yemen.

750 C.E.: Kaldi, or Khalid, observes the effect of coffee on goats and himself. The legend of Kaldi is most often shared as the story of the discovery of coffee.

Prior to 1000 A.D.: Galla, also known as Oromo, or free men of Ethiopia, the largest ethnic group in Ethiopia, use berries from coffee trees, ground up, and mixed with animal fat to give them energy during the day.

1000 A.D.: Arab traders carry coffee and domestication of the coffee plant begins. They also use boiled coffee to create a drink they call *qahwa*.

1453: Ottoman Turks carry coffee to Constantinople.

1475: Constantinople sees first coffee shop opened called Kiva Han.

1511: Khair Beg, a somewhat corrupt governor of Mecca, tries to ban coffee. He expresses fear that coffee drinkers would initiate a rebellion against him. The reigning sultan proclaims coffee sacred and executed the governor.

1607: Captain John Smith, a founder of the colony of Virginia, introduces coffee to North America.

1645: Italy sees its first coffeehouse, and coffee comes into general use in Italy. First coffeehouse opens in Venice. Some monks request Pope Clemente VIII to outlaw the Muslim brew. "He declines and says, "This beverage is so good it would be a sin to let only pagans drink it!" His subsequent "baptism" of coffee, quite simply, an unexpected full endorsement, propels its spread across Europe.

1652: England's first coffeehouse opens.

1668: Coffee surpasses beer as the preferred breakfast drink in New York City.

1668: Lloyds of London founder Edward Lloyd opens his coffeehouse in England, and many maritime insurance agents and merchants enjoy it. The coffeehouse becomes the famous Lloyds of London in subsequent years.

1670: Ottoman Turks control Yemen and any export of their prized coffee from the Yemeni Port of Mokha. Legend has it that Baba Budan, a pilgrim and a Moslem, smuggled seven seeds out by taping them to his stomach. Those seeds would be planted in India as the first.

1672: Paris enjoys its first coffeehouse.

1683: Franz Georg Kolschitzky, originally from Vienna who had lived in Turkey, uses the wartime spoils of the battle for Vienna with Turkey to open the first coffeehouse, named the Blue Bottle.

1690: The Dutch smuggle a coffee plant out of the Arab Port of Mokha and establish themselves as the first to move and cultivate coffee trade globally.

1715: Europe sees the construction of the first greenhouse built as home for the noble tree — the Arabica tree from which cuttings were used to foster new growth of billions of new trees, including most of what now is in Central and South America.

1721: The first coffeehouse opens in Berlin.

1727: Brazil is established as a coffee-growing region as a result of the smuggling of cuttings and seeds by Lieutenant Colonel Francisco de Melho Palheta, who served as an intermediary in a dispute with Dutch and French Guinea. He has an affair with the wife of the French Guinea governor. The bouquet of coffee is a departing gift.

1773: The Boston Tea Party happens, and coffee drinking gains notoriety as a patriotic drink in the United States.

1775: Frederick the Great in Prussia attempts to block trade of green coffee, but public sentiment prevents it.

1818: Laurens, a Parisian metalsmith, invents the first coffee percolator.

1860: James Folger establishes J.A. Folger Coffee Company in San Francisco.

1871: John Arbuckle invents a machine that fills, weighs, seals, and labels coffee in paper packages. From his factory in New York, the Arbuckle Ariosa became the first mass-produced coffee sold all over the United States.

1900: As the 20th century begins, Germans regularly enjoy afternoon coffee as a ritual and, conceivably, as a beverage.

1900: Hills Bros. packages the first vacuum pack tins of coffee, marking a decline in local roasting and coffee shops.

1901: Satori Kato, a Japanese American chemist living in Chicago, invents the first soluble instant coffee.

1901: Italian Luigi Bezzera invents a steam-driven high-speed extraction machine for coffee, and espresso is born.

1903: German researchers on behalf of German coffee importer Ludwig Roselius invent Sanka.

1906: George Constant Washington, an English chemist living in Guatemala, invents mass-produced instant coffee.

1920: U.S. Prohibition forces an increase in coffee sales.

1938: Nestlé invents freeze-dried coffee to support utilization of Brazil coffee crop surpluses. The result is Nescafé.

1940: Statistics indicate 70 percent of the world coffee crop ends up in the United States.

1942: World War II American soldiers are rationed Maxwell House coffee, and the United States sees hoarding, which forces rationing of coffee.

1946: Italian Achilles Gaggia perfects the espresso machine.

1966: Alfred Peet, driven by an awareness of the gap between widely available commercial coffee and higher quality, dark roasted specialty grade coffee, establishes Peets Coffee, Tea & Spices in Berkeley, California.

1971: Seattle Pike Place Public Market sees the first Starbucks, opened by Zev Siegl, Gordon Bowker, and Jerry Baldwin, three young entrepreneurs. Starbucks Coffee, Tea & Spices is a dry goods business and sells coffee, tea, and spices but not beverages.

1995: Doug and Emily Zell found Intelligentsia Coffee in Chicago.

1995: Brett Smith and Fred Houk, two University of North Carolina business school friends, found Counter Culture Coffee in Durham, North Carolina.

1999: Duane Sorenson founds Stumptown Coffee in Portland, Oregon.

2002: Trish Rothgeb, cofounder of Wrecking Ball coffee in San Francisco, coins the term "Third Wave," when asked about the business of coffee in an interview. The description notes a new emphasis on quality that would define this era and carry into today.

2002: James Freeman founds Blue Bottle Coffee in Oakland.

2012: JAB holding, a Luxembourg-based private company, acquires Peets Coffee & Tea, and six months after that acquisition purchases Caribou Coffee, a Minnesota-based chain with more than 400 stores.

2013: JAB purchases D.E Master Blenders 1753.

2013: University of California, Davis, opens the UC Davis Coffee Center, the first multidisciplinary university research center to address the challenges and needs of the coffee industry using a holistic approach to coffee science and education.

2015: JAB becomes Jacobs Douwe Egberts (JDE). JDE merges with Mondelez International Coffee Company shortly thereafter.

2015: Peets Coffee acquires both Stumptown and Intelligentsia.

2015: JDE acquires Nordic coffee chain Espresso House, which then acquires German coffee shop chain Balzac Coffee.

2015: JDE continues a Nordic focus by acquiring Denmark's largest coffee shop chain, Baresso Coffee.

2015: The Sustainable Coffee Challenge is created. Conceived by Conservation International and Starbucks, it's a collaborative effort by companies, governments, NGOs, research institutions, and others to transition the coffee sector to be fully sustainable.

2016: JDE acquires Green Mountain Coffee.

2017: Nestlé purchases 68 percent controlling stake in Oakland's Blue Bottle coffee.

2018: JDE invests in TRADE, a new coffee-focused e-trading platform that offers personalized recommendations of more than 350 specialty roasts.

2018: Agnieszka Rojewska becomes the first woman to win the World Barista Championship.

2019: Nestlé pays Starbucks $7.15 billion to acquire exclusive rights to sell its coffee and teas.

Index

N